P9-DWR-634

Renata Tebaldi

Tebaldi as Adriana Lecouvreur.

Renata Tebaldi

by Kenn Harris

Drake Publishers Inc.
New York

Published in 1974 by
Drake Publishers Inc.
381 Park Avenue South
New York, New York 10016

Library of Congress Cataloging in Publication Data
Harris, Kenn, 1947-
Renata Tebaldi; an authorized biography.
Discography: p.
1. Tebaldi, Renata.
ML420.T28H3 782.1'092'4 (B) 73-18069

ISBN 0-87749-597-1

Frontispiece: Renata Tebaldi as Adriana Lecouvreur
(Photo by Max Waldman)

Printed in the United States of America

In memory of my grandmother, Rose Zimble, whose unwavering faith always made me so proud.

Table of Contents

Preface

New York City: Friday, February 25, 1972, 6 P.M. A crowd had gathered in the drafty, underground passageway in front of the stage entrance to the Metropolitan Opera House. A chilly rain had been falling all day long, and the air was uncomfortably drafty in the Lincoln Center vehicular tunnel. Yet upwards of fifty people were waiting patiently, many holding bouquets and small, gift-wrapped packages. The occasion? The opera *Falstaff* was to be presented at the Met that evening, for the first time in several seasons. However welcome the revival of Verdi's comic masterpiece, and even given the presence of Sir Geraint Evans in the title role, Regina Resnik as Mistress Quickly, and Kostas Paskalis as Master Ford, there was still a specially festive aura reflected in the faces of the stage door throng that these elements alone could not have kindled. The reason, of course, was that the role of Mistress Alice Ford would be sung that night by Renata Tebaldi.

Tebaldi was making her first New York appearance in fourteen months. She had not been heard at the Met since an incredibly moving performance of *Andrea Chenier* on December 28, 1970, and, in fact, the soprano had made no appearances since singing Desdemona in *Otello* on January 5, 1971 in Philadelphia. Clearly, this was an "occasion." But then, to large numbers of fans at the Met and elsewhere, every Tebaldi performance was a highlight of a musical season. The Metropolitan's roster in those days abounded with international "superstars," each of whom had hordes of admirers, but the crowds that braved the elements to greet Tebaldi before and after every performance surpassed even the Nilsson and Corelli fans in sheer numbers.

There was, to be sure, a note of poignancy, as well as expectation, in the air. Tebaldi's previous Met appearances, in the fall of 1970 in *Chenier,* had on several occasions been marked by some singing that had not been comparable to her best work in the recent past. Everyone hoped that the months of rest and study would have returned the soprano to top form. There was also eagerness to see Renata in a role new to her New York public. All these considerations were pushed aside as the sleek limousine provided by London Records pulled up to the stage door. As Tebaldi was helped from the car, the cheering began, cries of "Brava, Renata!" filled the air. Tebaldi, always glad to see her fans, was clearly touched by the greeting, and, while she smiled, waved, and greeted a number of people by name, tears were not far away. Finally, laden with the flowers and trinkets offered by the assembled greeting party, Tebaldi was allowed to make her way backstage to prepare for the performance, while the rest of us went to dinner, or simply gathered inside the Met's lobby waiting for eight o'clock.

Falstaff is an antidiva opera! The title role is sung by a baritone and there are four major roles for women. Indeed, this opera requires a superior ensemble, not merely a number of brilliant singers working independently of one another. Even so, many in the audience that evening were "guilty" of caring more about Mistress Ford than for anything or anyone else in the opera! Although the first scene of the opera crackled with humor and glowed with Evans' spirited performance, many of us could hardly concentrate on it. After a twenty-minute "eternity," the second scene, set in Mistress Ford's garden, began. As the curtain rose and the four "merry wives of Windsor" entered, the applause built up until there was a full-fledged roar of adoration for Tebaldi. Although Tebaldi made every attempt to continue the scene, her colleague Joann Grillo, singing Meg Page, firmly led her downstage to acknowledge the cheering and then turned away, leaving the action frozen for several moments until the ovation faded away. For the first time in anyone's memory a scene had to be begun again, for the welcome was so vociferous that the orchestra lost its place. From there on, the evening went smoothly, with each artist giving his or her best, Tebaldi delighted the audience with her grace of gesture, her flair for comedy, and the freshness of her singing, and, as called for in the score, she capped the evening with a triumphant high C in the finale. The entire performance was joyously received by the audience. The 1971-72 season was Sir Rudolf Bing's last as general manager, and he had put together some of the soundest, most glamorous casts of his entire administration. Even in the illustrious company of Bing's *La Fille du Regiment* and *Tristan;* however, this *Falstaff* was a major event.

After the performance, the throng at the stage door was even more excited than earlier. After emerging from the opera house, Tebaldi spent the better part of the next hour seated inside her automobile, signing autographs, accepting still more flowers and gifts, and holding brief but friendly conversations with the dozens of fans who waited for their moment with her to arrive. It wasn't until one in the morning that Tebaldi was "allowed" by her friends to return to her apartment!

Readers of this book not acquainted with the phenomenon of Tebaldi's singing, who have never heard her in a live performance or even on records, may ask what all the excitement is about. Is Tebaldi not just one of many opera stars, a chic prima donna with her fan club, her strong points and weaknesses on stage? To these people I suggest that before, or even while, reading any further, they obtain a Tebaldi record and play it, to sample for themselves the glorious voice of Renata Tebaldi. My book, intended as a chronicle of Tebaldi's career, can describe events through words and pictures, but only Tebaldi herself can document these words with her song. It is one thing to state that hers is one of the two or three most beautiful voices known in this century, and that her stage presence is one of the most extraordinary in current experience; but only Tebaldi's work in the opera house or on discs can lend credence to these statements.

Those whose lives have been immeasurably enriched by Tebaldi's music will, I hope, find in these pages a valid and meaningful appraisal of her artistry as preserved on discs, in tapes of performances, and in the memory of those who attended her performances in the opera house or on the concert stage.

There are some artists whom the public holds in great if remote awe. Their artistry is venerated but the artists themselves seem inaccessible, immune to human concern. Others—Caruso, for example—are very human, and the admiration one holds for their singing is mixed with that most human of feelings, love. It is to this group that Renata Tebaldi most certainly belongs. As all who have seen her in person know, the love that is sent to her by the audience is returned by Tebaldi. The cheering crowds who stand and holler "Brava, Renata" can see the tears of happiness in Renata's eyes as she acknowledges their applause, and feel swept up in those gestures of affection that Tebaldi always offers. Those who know Renata Tebaldi personally can attest to the simple charm, tact, consideration, and unaffected pleasantness that characterize her.

This book is offered as a tribute to a superb artist and a delightful, warm person, who has created with her singing a special and more beautiful world.

Acknowledgments

I would like to express my gratitude to the many friends and associates whose help and encouragement made this book possible: To Sir Rudolf Bing, Mr. Francis Robinson, and Miss Tina Vigano, who gave generously of their time; to Mr. T. A. McEwen, who gave wise counsel; to Miss Lois Kirschenbaum, who provided many of the candid photographs found within these pages and who also was a tireless source of detailed operatic lore; to Louise St. Laurent for the photos which she contributed; and to Miss Nelly Walter of Columbia Artists Management, Inc.

To my friends who cheered me when my typewriter faltered and my nerves threatened to snap, a heartfelt token of my appreciation: *mille grazie* to staunch *Tebaldiani* Paul C. Brynan, Thomas S. Simpson, Janet Carey, et al.; to my editor, Harvey Silbert; and to dear friends Gillian Hyde, Bruce Zemsky, Carl Saslow, Eugene Klein, Jeffrey Golland, Marsh Boyler, Clyde Putallaz, Todd Lichtenstein, Richard Sherr, Georgie Railley, Linda Sirkus, Cherry Munson, Joe Bartomioli, Howard Hankin, Ted Modrik, and many more.

Very special thanks to those indefatigable aural historians Alan Fischer and Ed Rosen, whose outstanding tapes and vintage recordings were of great help to me and which document so brilliantly the artistry of Renata Tebaldi.

Last but not least, thanks to my parents, George and Marion Harris, and such kith and kin as Lucille, Norman, and Harriet Cooper, Fay Jacobs, and Gwen Rubenstein.

Tebaldi as Marguerite in *Faust* (1947).

Renata Tebaldi

Recondita armonia

In the late spring of 1973, when I met with Renata Tebaldi to begin work on this book, I could not help being struck by the distances, both physical and metaphorical, the soprano had traveled in her life. Born in Pesaro, a small town in Italy, Tebaldi had sung in virtually every major city in Europe, the Americas, and Japan. The shy young girl who had journeyed to Milan with her mother in order to audition for Arturo Toscanini after World War II had since become a major musical figure herself, who, in common with the great maestro, represented musical achievement of the first degree. The naturally pretty woman who, at the beginning of her career, favored simple coiffures and modest clothing had transformed herself into a radiantly elegant prima donna. Her originally stately and reserved stage demeanor had ripened into a fiery and commanding presence.

I did not, of course, know Renata Tebaldi as she was growing up in Pesaro, nor even in her first years as a professional singer, and therefore I do not personally know how, if at all, she herself has changed through the years. However, I have been able to observe her easy, ready kindness, her loyalty to friends, her disarming sense of humor, and even, once in a while, flashes of anger. I suspect that these qualities have always been hers, for her graciousness is always totally direct and her impatience, when demonstrated, is devoid of staginess. Loyalty to friends, dignity in the face of the less friendly, and devotion to hard work must have been naturally ingrained in Tebaldi from childhood.

Born on February 1, 1922 in Pesaro, Tebaldi grew up with her mother, Giuseppina Tebaldi, in the home of her maternal grandparents. The soprano's father, Teobaldo Tebaldi, was a cellist who had separated from her mother before Renata's birth. Her mother thought it best to withhold the true circumstances surrounding her husband's departure from her only daughter, and Renata believed that her father was dead until fellow pupils in her primary school class told her otherwise. From her mother Renata found out her father's address and began writing him. Evidently the elder Tebaldi was delighted to find that his daughter was interested in him. He replied to her letters, invited her to visit him, and eventually reconciled with his wife and rejoined his family. The reconciliation lasted none too long, and after a number of months Tebaldi's parents separated once more, this time permanently.

Although Renata was saddened by this further rupture of her family life, she still of course had her mother and her grandparents to turn to for love, and she was increasingly occupied by her schoolwork and her study of the piano. Stricken with polio at the age of three, the lingering effects of the ailment prevented her from enjoying much outdoor play with other children. How fortunate that her affinity for music became apparent at an early age.

By her early teens, Renata was a serious and diligent student of the piano, and thought vaguely of a career as a teacher, if not a performer, of music. In her spare time, she sang, too . . . In fact, Renata became so enamored with singing that she soon grew impatient with her piano lessons, which were made bearable only because they were given by a cousin she adored, and who also let Renata sing for her occasionally.

Over the objections of her mother, who was skeptical of the

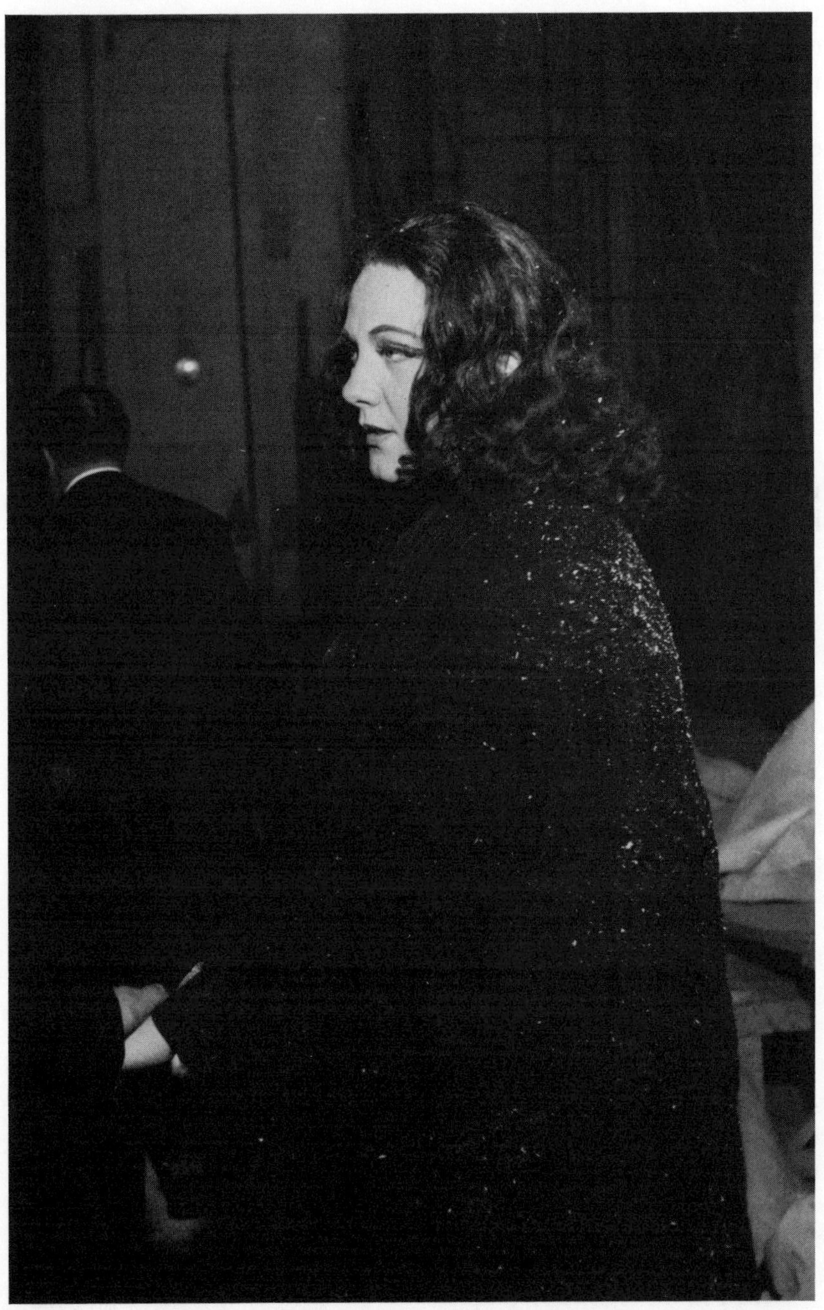

Tebaldi as Catalani's *La Wally* at La Scala in 1955.

idea, Renata began to take voice lessons at the Conservatory of Parma, where she studied with Ettore Campogaliani, a well-respected teacher. His students also included tenor Gino Penna and a young baritone named Carlo Bergonzi, who eventually metamorphosized into the finest lyric Italian tenor of his generation and also became a frequent colleague of Tebaldi's in opera houses and on recordings.

Renata studied with Maestro Campogaliani for three years. Then, when she was eighteen years old, she was invited to spend Christmas in Pesaro with some relatives. During her visit Renata was prevailed upon by her aunt to sing for the family. The aunt was sufficiently impressed with her young niece's voice to contact an acquaintance who had been a famous opera singer and currently taught at the local conservatory. That acquaintance was Carmen Melis, who had been hailed throughout her long career in Europe and the Americas as a masterful interpreter of such roles as Tosca, Minnie in *La Fanciulla del West*, Thais, and the title role of Riccardo Zandonai's opera *Francesca da Rimini.*

Zandonai, who was widely respected as both a teacher and a composer of operas and songs, was then a teaching colleague of Melis' at the Pesaro Conservatory. While Renata was still on her holiday visit it was arranged that she would sing for both Melis and Zandonai. As Tebaldi proudly recalls, both of her celebrated auditors were immediately aware of her superior talent as a singer. Melis advised her to concentrate on voice, and agreed to take Renata on as a student if she was willing to move to Pesaro. This was a fortunate step for both, for in Melis Tebaldi found an excellent mentor who prepared her for the Verdi, Puccini, and *verismo* roles that were to form the basis of her repertoire, and in Tebaldi Melis found her most brilliant disciple, who in her own successes would perpetuate Melis' name as well as her prowess as a teacher and standard bearer of the Italian operatic tradition.

Tebaldi studied with Melis in Pesaro for three years. Her work was arduous, but Tebaldi applied herself diligently, strengthening her technique and learning repertoire. The technique that Melis imparted to Tebaldi was sound, allowing her to develop a soprano voice with unprecedented strength and clarity, and a silken purity of tone for two octaves or more. Melis led Tebaldi in the direction of the later Verdi and such composers as Puccini, Giordano, and Cilea. Melis did not aim to make Tebaldi into a coloratura specialist, correctly surmising that given the prodigious size of her voice she would make her mark as a *lirico spinto* soprano.

In spite of this excellent progress, all was not easy for the young soprano. For one thing, her mother was doubtful that Renata's singing career would take wing—how far away the stages of the great opera houses must have seemed to Signora Giuseppina! Also, Italy was deep in the throes of World War II, which by 1942 was going quite badly for the Italians. Allied bombings forced the close of the Pesaro Conservatory in that year. Leaving Pesaro for the relative safety of the countryside, Renata continued her studies alone, following the maxims and technique that Melis and Zandonai had taught her. Times were brightened whenever she received letters from these two musicians, who had taken her under their artistic protection. In one sense, though, Tebaldi was fortunate in having to study alone—this brought out her own self-critical faculties and developed the sense of discipline that in future years helped her to restudy technique and individual scores by herself.

By 1944, Mussolini had fallen and the worst of the war was over for the Italians. As life slowly returned to normal, opera houses began to reopen. Although La Scala had been practically destroyed by Allied bombing, a number of the smaller theatres were in operation. Carmen Melis had contacts with various managements, and in early 1944 was able to secure a debut role for Tebaldi at the opera house in Rovigo. The opera was Boito's *Mefistofele* and the role was Elena (Helen of Troy). Elena is a brief role, subordinate in musical and dramatic importance to Margherita. While Margherita has two scenes and the aria "L'altra notte in fondo al mare," Elena has but one scene, the Walpurgisnacht, in which she and Faust sing a passionate love duet. Still, the part calls for warm, vibrant singing, and the grandly melodious vocal line is one of the most memorable components of Boito's opera. It was by no means an inauspicious role for a professional debut.

One wonders how many in the audience who heard Renata Tebaldi that night in Rovigo realized that they were not only hearing an extraordinary voice, but witnessing the debut of an artist destined for a career of almost unparalleled glory. The opera houses of provincial Italy are filled with young artists beginning their careers, as well as experienced singers who have not made great names for themselves in the more renowned operatic centers. Performances in such theatres are often exciting but somewhat ragged musically. Of course, there is nothing like the thrill that opera buffs experience at such a performance when one artist, young and unknown, rises above the inelegant surroundings to offer singing far beyond what one would expect to hear under the circumstances. There must have been many in the *Mefistofele* audience who made mental notes to follow the career of the young Elena of that evening.

Although her debut was accomplished, Tebaldi returned to her studies at once. But she now knew she could survive the ordeal of appearing on a stage and facing an audience of strangers. Tebaldi quite naturally had been nervous that evening, but she never lost her composure, and, as she recalls, she lost her fears once her music started and she began to sing.

In a sense, the debut was a sort of dress rehearsal for future engagements. Renata did not sing again publicly for a year. Her next appearance was in Trieste, where she sang her first performance of a role that was to become one of her very finest: Desdemona in Verdi's *Otello*. After this performance, Tebaldi began to receive offers from opera houses throughout Italy, and she soon found herself fulfilling engagements in Brescia, Parma, and elsewhere, singing *Otello*, *La Bohème*, and so on. By mid-1946 she was rapidly gaining in experience, her performances taking on ever more assurance and poise. Tebaldi was singing, and singing leading roles. Unfortunately, her engagements in the smaller theatres brought her few rewards beyond the opportunity to perform before an audience.

Salaries were terribly low, and she had yet to sing in a major production anywhere.

Meanwhile, the operatic world in Italy and elsewhere was preparing itself for a major event—the reopening of the rebuilt La Scala Opera House. Its bombing was one of the senseless tragedies of the war. Though of no strategic importance in itself, the opera house is located in the center of Milan, the industrial capital of Italy, so that its destruction was almost inevitable. Somehow the postwar Italian government found the funds for the rebuilding of La Scala (fortunately, the contents of La Scala's museum had been crated away and escaped damage), and Arturo Toscanini, a steadfast foe of the Mussolini government who had refused to work in Italy while the fascists were in power, had agreed to return to his native land to conduct the opening concert.

Toscanini was then 78 years old. His brilliance as a conductor was as legendary as the fear he inspired in musicians who would not or could not meet the extraordinary standards he set. This man, who as a youth of twenty had played second cello at the first performance of *Otello* (also at La Scala), who had been an intimate friend of Giacomo Puccini and had conducted the world premieres of *La Bohème, La Fanciulla del West,* and *Turandot,* who had led performances of Wagnerian operas and the symphonies of Beethoven and Brahms, was revered as a link to the greatest flowering of Italian opera. His undertaking the direction of La Scala's reopening gave the event even greater significance than it would otherwise have had.

Toscanini announced his intention of seeking out fresh, young vocal talent and began holding auditions at La Scala. In addition to being personally interested in finding new talent, Toscanini was performing a great service to the Italian operatic public, as the mid-forties were not notable for great singers in Italy. Gigli was past his prime, as was Ebe Stignani, although both were still capable of imposing work. Pinza and Albanese spent the war years in the United States, during which time they had gone to the forefront of the Metropolitan Opera roster. Muzio had died, and the leading dramatic soprano in Italy was Maria Caniglia, a lady with a large and rather metallic voice who had been leading soprano at the Rome Opera for nearly two decades, excelling in such Verdian roles as Aïda, Leonora in *Forza*, and Amelia in *Un Ballo in Maschera*, as well as the heroines of *Tosca*, *Fedora*, and *Chenier*. Caniglia made her greatest points through force of personality and a simple, undisciplined style of singing. She was a much adored artist and demonstrably fine singer; on vocal terms alone, though, she was less than awe-inspiring.

Clearly, then, there was a need for gifted young singers. Among those who began to emerge in those first postwar years in Italy were tenors Giuseppe di Stefano and Mario del Monaco, baritones Ettore Bastianini and Carlo Bergonzi (he would not switch to the tenor repertoire until 1951), and basses Nicolai Rossi-Lemeni and Cesare Siepi. Tito Gobbi and Giulietta Simionato had begun singing before the war, advancing from comprimario parts to leading roles in the postwar years. A Greek-American soprano destined to play a major role in the postwar operatic renaissance in Italy, Maria Callas, was yet to appear on the horizon.

Tebaldi, who wanted desperately to sing before Toscanini, realized that without contacts in his circle of acquaintances she had little chance to do so. What she did not know was that someone who knew the conductor had heard her sing and had recommended that Toscanini hear the young and unknown soprano. Thus Tebaldi received word that Toscanini wished her to audition for him. Excited beyond belief, the soprano replied immediately and an appointment was arranged. Tebaldi and her mother traveled to Milan.

On the appointed morning, Tebaldi walked from the *pensione* where she and her mother were staying to the opera house. After what seemed like an eternity of waiting, Renata heard a secretary call "Signor Renato Tebaldi, please." A clerical error had caused Toscanini to expect a young man named Tebaldi to sing for him. Embarrassed and confused, and wondering if the maestro was interested in hearing a soprano at all that day, Tebaldi stepped forward. Everyone, including the maestro, smiled as the error was revealed to them. Then Toscanini asked Tebaldi what she would sing. She had prepared "La mamma morta" from *Andrea Chenier,* Desdemona's "Willow Song" and "Ave Maria" from *Otello.* She sang these pieces for Toscanini, and she must have sung especially well that day, for Toscanini was, in her words, "very enthusiastic" and told Ghiringhelli, La Scala's director, who was also present, that he was sure she would bring him, and La Scala, great satisfaction. Renata was engaged for the opening concert, and was to remain on the La Scala roster for more than a decade. At the concert Tebaldi sang the "Prayer" from Rossini's biblical opera *Mose,* and the soprano part in Verdi's *Te Deum.* Among the other soloists that evening was the young bass Cesare Siepi. An anti-Mussolini partisan, Siepi had spent much of the war in hiding, and, like Tebaldi, was only beginning to become a familiar personality to operagoers.

After the La Scala debut, Tebaldi began to sing in the major opera houses, singing roles that would become her "standard repertoire" in Milan, Venice, Naples, Trieste, and elsewhere. At La Scala, where she soon became a leading soprano, Tebaldi also sang the role of Eva in Wagner's *I Maestri Cantori di Nuremburg* (known otherwise as *Die Meistersinger*). In Naples she sang Elsa in *Lohengrin* and Elisabeth in *Tannhäuser,* all in Italian. A tape of a Naples *Lohengrin* survives, and Tebaldi recorded arias from Tannhäuser, Lohengrin, and even Isolde's Liebestod, again in Italian, as part of the *Tebaldi Festival* album in 1969.

The *Lohengrin* tape reveals her as a lyrical embodiment of the simple Elsa. *Lohengrin* is one of Wagner's operas that lies close to the Italian tradition, and Tebaldi performs the music naturally and with ease.

Among the surprising roles that Tebaldi performed in the first years of her career were Cleopatra in Handel's *Giulio Cesare* and Pamira in Rossini's *L'Assedio di Corinto*—this last at the Florence May Festival. The Teatro Fenice in Venice revived Verdi's seldom performed *Giovanna d'Arco* for Tebaldi, and she had a great success in the title role, Joan of Arc. In Verdi's opera, Joan falls in love with Carlo, the Dauphin, and Verdi gave these unlikely lovers a spirited duet. Carlo was sung by

Carlo Bergonzi, who had recently become a tenor. The production was eventually transported to Paris, where Tebaldi scored a major triumph in an opera that French audiences always have despised for the bizarre liberties taken with St. Joan's character.

In 1950 La Scala presented Tebaldi to British audiences for the first time during a guest engagement at Covent Garden, in which she sang in *Otello* and Verdi's *Requiem*, and later staged a new production of *La Traviata* for her. Although some reservations were expressed concerning a certain coolness in her interpretation of Violetta, people flocked to hear her in the role.

Tebaldi had to cancel one performance of *Traviata* in 1951, because of illness. Unable to locate a suitable Violetta from within the La Scala company, Ghiringhelli cabled a young foreign artist whom he had heard as Gioconda in Verona in 1947. In the interim she had married an Italian millionaire and had performed a startling variety of roles—Abagaille, Isolde, Brünnhilde in *Die Walküre*, and Lucia. The singer was Maria Callas. Callas, then a heavy young woman with an imposing voice and a sense of dramatic conviction soon to be as famous offstage as on, agreed to make her debut under these somewhat inauspicious circumstances. Eventually she was rewarded with a Scala contract of her own . . .

Meanwhile, Tebaldi recovered and continued to sing at La Scala and elsewhere, making her American debut at the San Francisco Opera as *Aïda*, with Mario Del Monaco singing Rhadames.

With its acquisition of Callas, La Scala soon found itself in the lucky position of being able to command the services of the two most popular sopranos of the day. At that time Callas and Tebaldi seemed to have maintained certain friendly feelings for each other. Each had her own partisans, but the rivalry between them had not yet become distorted by the press or the ladies' most fanatical admirers. Thus, by 1953, La Scala was able to open with *La Wally* starring Tebaldi in the title role (Renata Scotto sang Walter in that production) and then present Callas in the title role of *La Sonnambula* a night or two later, with Bernstein conducting. If this does not represent a "Golden Age," what does?

With her La Scala visit to London and Edinburgh, her trip to Paris for *Giovanna d'Arco,* and her San Francisco debut as Aïda, Tebaldi's career began to take on an international aura. In 1948, Tebaldi had signed a recording contract with Decca-London, and, after several initial releases of arias (discussed in more detail in the "Recordings" section of this book), the company took advantage of the recent development of long-playing records to begin recording her in complete operas, including *Aïda, Bohème, Tosca, Otello,* and *Madama Butterfly.* These recordings, released all over the world, brought Tebaldi international fame well in advance of personal appearances.

Tebaldi began singing each season in Latin America, where in Brazil her path crossed that of her Scala colleague, Maria Meneghini Callas. (The story of their entanglement there and the subsequent "feud" is recounted in the next chapter.)

By the time of her Metropolitan debut, in 1955, Tebaldi had sung in virtually every operatic capitol (Vienna was still to come). From 1955 through 1960, she divided her time between the United States, La Scala, and the Teatro San Carlo in Naples, with guest appearances elsewhere.

One of the negative results of the contretemps between Tebaldi and Callas was the inability of La Scala's Ghiringhelli to keep both divas on his roster. Tebaldi, who had had several opening nights at La Scala, including the Toscanini concert in 1946, looked on and saw that the now svelte and glamorous Callas was being given opening nights and new productions each season, while she herself was being offered less and less of interest.

Without denying the fact that the early and middle 1950s were Callas's greatest years, filled with magnificent achievements, it does seem ludicrous in retrospect that a theatre like La Scala had to become lopsided in its favors, with its director catering to Callas, whose reputation for temperament threatened to exceed the renown of her singing, at the expense of Tebaldi. Each soprano had a large group of partisans, who not only bravaed their respective heroines but often deluged the rival lady with boos, obscene letters and telephone calls. Tebaldi, who generally maintained an attitude of dignified silence when it came to sparring with Callas, decided to leave La Scala for a while after 1959. Ironically, Ghiringhelli could not retain Callas's services for very long after Tebaldi's departure. They quarreled, and Callas left with some bitterness in the early 1960s. Milan's citizenry thus found itself deprived of both of its *dive supreme,* with both "La Sublime" (the fans' nickname for Tebaldi) and "La Divina" (Callas) in "exile." (In truth, La Scala has yet to recover from the loss of the two singers, as no one has filled their respective places within the company.)

Having left La Scala, Tebaldi began to find herself in the United States for increasingly long periods of time, and grew to consider New York a second home. Traveling with her daughter throughout the career she had grown to believe in and cherish, Tebaldi's mother had helped make her feel at home in each new city. After her mother's death in 1957 (see "The Metropolitan Years") Tebaldi began to rely more and more on the friendship and housekeeping of Ernestina "Tina" Vigano. Tina because Tebaldi's dresser, confidant, and cook, and proved herself to be a loyal friend as well. Tina, who had thoroughly mastered English before Tebaldi became fluent, saw to it that the backstage crowds did not crush the diva in their enthusiasm, and she remained at Tebaldi's side dispensing photographs for Tebaldi to sign and give to the throngs who came to greet her. A lifelong opera buff, Tina has efficiently run Tebaldi's schedule, keeping her household in order wherever she sings. A warm and tactful person, the diminutive Tina is almost as admired by Tebaldi's friends and fans as is the soprano herself.

After the death of her mother, Tebaldi became reconciled to her father. Although the elder Tebaldi had seen his daughter in the opera house numerous times, she resisted renewing contact with him. After her mother passed away, however, Tebaldi realized that it was wrong to deprive herself of her father's love and to deprive him of the affection of his only daughter. The bond between them, never completely broken, was eventually healed, and although Tebaldi and her father were never as close as the soprano and her mother, they remained on excellent terms until Teobaldo Tebaldi's death in 1967.

Renata Tebaldi lives today in a sunny apartment on Manhattan's West Side. When in Italy, she lives in an apartment which she has maintained in Milan for many years. The Milanese flat houses Tebaldi's large collection of jade pieces, of which she is justly proud. Her New York residence, plushly carpeted in green, is more simply furnished.

Much has been written of Tebaldi the artist, Tebaldi the diva. What is Tebaldi like as a private individual? She lives quietly, and she is more likely to be discovered browsing in the shops on Fifth Avenue than at a Broadway opening night or even in an opera audience, although she enjoys the theatre. The soprano works hard at her art, studying and practicing each day. Tebaldi often describes herself as shy, and on some occasions her reserve is seen as aloofness, although this could not be further from the truth. What has always impressed me about Tebaldi is her complete lack of false or fancy airs. On being introduced, she takes her visitor's hand firmly in her own and greets him in Italian or English. Her smile is ready and unforced, and she laughs heartily at jokes. Casual backstage visitors occasionally pose thoughtless questions, and these are politely and tactfully responded to. More serious questions about repertoire on future plans are usually answered frankly.

The nature of her profession dictates that Tebaldi watch her health very carefully. Instrumentalists can perform with a cold or sore throat, but to a singer even a minor indisposition can result in several cancelled appearances. Therefore Tebaldi seldom goes out or speaks much on the day of a performance. Although she admits to some nervousness before a performance, Tebaldi vanquishes such nerves by the time she steps out on the stage. Tebaldi's great concentration is apparent not only while the opera is going on, but also during the curtain calls. Although she'll smile and wave during these bows, one senses her feeling that all is not yet finished. A certain tension makes one aware of the double identity of the artist—the individual whom one knows and admires, and the performer eager to go on with the opera, remaining at least partly in character even during the act breaks.

Once the opera ends, the tension is gone. Tebaldi stands before her audience responding to their cheers with her smile and her curtain call "trademark," stretching out both arms and rapidly opening and closing her hands, which in her native area means "I will come back!" Backstage, Tebaldi is invariably cordial, even exuberant, when friends enter her dressing room to say hello after the opera.

What is always remarkable about Tebaldi's backstage demeanor is that, even with a dressing room full of guests, including good friends and fans, she always pays attention to what is being said to her. When others might simply smile and say a benign "Yes" or "thank you" to everything, Tebaldi listens to a whole statement and then replies in kind. She has worked diligently on her English and is now quite fluent.

Tebaldi enjoys talking about her work and her roles, often dispelling myths that have cropped up about herself as she goes along. For instance, while some people see Desdemona as her best role, Tebaldi states that it is not her favorite, as she is bothered by the character's relative passivity. She therefore seizes gratefully on the opportunities offered in the third act to show some force of personality and a touch of defiance to the raging Otello. Similarly, in the fourth act, Tebaldi allows us to see Desdemona's terror and heartbreak, thereby relieving the heroine, whom Tebaldi calls "a sweet woman," of some of her blandness. Tebaldi, who always studies the sources of the libretti of her roles, is aware that Shakespeare's Desdemona, unlike Boito's and Verdi's, is a witty and almost vixenish young girl who enjoys teasing her husband. Although the point is somewhat obscured in the opera, which omits Shakespeare's first act, Desdemona is also brave enough to defy her father and elope with Otello. One sees these elements of her character incorporated into Tebaldi's Desdemona.

Tebaldi avows that she has great feeling for all the roles that have become part of her repertoire, and admits to involving herself greatly in each performance—"Every time I sing, I leave a piece of my heart on stage."

While learning a new role, Tebaldi learns the words and music together. To learn them separately, she feels would be wrong, since the words are illuminated by the music. Studying them together enables her to create a character in which words and music are inseparable. Thus, in her view, her interpretations are well integrated, with words and music properly balanced.

Tebaldi has always found the role of Adriana Lecouvreur very congenial, although many critics despise Cilea's opera and disparage companies that revive it. As a performer, Tebaldi sees the role as offering her the chance to do a great deal of acting, allowing her to show her loving, gentle side in the scenes with Maurizio, and her power as an actress in her encounter with the Princess de Bouillion (the mezzo-soprano role). Furthermore, in the performing of the denunciation scene from Racine's *Phèdre* in the third act, the soprano has a brief but important fling at the authentic style of the French *tragédienne* on whose life the opera is (loosely) based. The fourth act offers Tebaldi the challenge of Adriana's taxing death scene, in which her physical agony must be represented, as well as the "romantic" tragedy of love thwarted by the evil action of another person. Adriana's final, delirious moments must, according to Tebaldi, be given an "angelic" quality.

Among the roles which Tebaldi sees as giving her the most opportunity to act are Aïda, Violetta, and Manon Lescaut. Aïda, according to the soprano, must show how she is being torn apart by the opposing forces of her loyalty to her country and her love for Radames. In particular, says Tebaldi, "Aïda must show that she is very much in love with Radames."

Violetta in *La Traviata* is special to Tebaldi, because the character is so delicate, and yet so strong in her love for Alfredo that she can sacrifice herself even to the extent of pretending in the third act that she loves the baron.

Manon Lescaut, in the soprano's view, is basically an innocent creature who falls in love too early, when she is unable to handle the situation. She becomes involved with Des Grieux when she is still coquettish, thus falling into trouble.

Another Puccini heroine who has figured greatly in Tebaldi's career is Mimi in *La Bohème*, whom she sees as innocent and romantic, yet clever and very "real." Tebaldi says she feels somehow very close to Mimi when she sings the role.

Tebaldi sees acting as only very slightly subordinate to the musical demands of her roles. She feels that the stage director and singers should collaborate closely on the creation of an operatic performance, but she is very much against blindly following a director's idea if it runs counter to the demands of the music. Tebaldi, who has developed her own insight into her characters over the years, says that she enjoys very much offering her own opinions to a director in the spirit of working toward a successful performance.

Tebaldi first began singing under the Italian *stagione* system, in which a group of artists are engaged to sing one opera at a time, singing all scheduled performances in a period of a few weeks.During her Metropolitan years she has had to contend with the Met's repertory system, in which operas are presented throughout a long season, with frequent changes of casts. At the Met, Tebaldi might sing six Toscas a season, and face a different tenor and baritone at each performance. Tebaldi prefers the *stagione* system because it enables the acting to become integrated and more detailed as the performers learn to react to each other's interpretations.

Tebaldi has been faced with some difficult moments onstage caused by accidents or errors. In particular, she recalls a performance of *Tosca* in Dallas during which the stagehands forgot to place lighted candles on Scarpia's desk in the second act. Tosca, after killing Scarpia, is called upon by the libretto to place a candle at either side of the dead man's head. The murder scene is one of the most powerful moments in all opera, and Puccini's music underscores each detail of the crime, including the moment when Tosca places those candles. To eliminate this moment would greatly diminish the effect of the scene. Thinking quickly, Tebaldi decided to use candles from a large candelabra which illuminated the scene. The action worked, the scene was as spine-tingling as ever, and, as the soprano remembers very happily, the next day all the reviews commented on her unusual variation on the traditional action, which saved the scene!

Although Tebaldi has never herself been one to indulge in practical jokes onstage, she is able to take them. One season, several years ago, Tebaldi was singing Mimi at the Metropolitan. Alcindoro was being sung by the inimitable buffo, Fer-Bing gave the opera in a new and heavily cut production in 1952. This production has always been popular with Metropolitan audiences, and the 1956 performances, which matched Tebaldi with Tucker, Warren, Corena, and Hines, were sold out and, to judge from accounts of those present, memorable.
contrived to be playing with a squirting seltzer bottle during Musetta's Waltz. Moments after that celebrated aria, Musetta, in order to send the old fellow away, pretends that her shoe is pinching and begins to scream with supposed anguish. At precisely that moment, Corena, pretending to be startled, lost control of the seltzer bottle and squirted a fair amount of the liquid not at Clarice Carson, the Musetta of that afternoon, but at Tebaldi, sitting close by as Mimi. Of course the audience howled with laughter, and if Tebaldi minded, she never let on. Instead, as Mimi, she joined in the general merriment!

As this book is written, Renata Tebaldi can look back on her career thus far and say that she has been able to sing nearly every role that has caught her interest. When I asked her if there were any roles she had never sung but wanted to, or that she thought she might perform one day, her answer was affirmative. She reminded me that although she has studied Massenet's *Manon*, and recorded two of Manon's arias, she has not actually sung it onstage. She also hopes to perform another Massenet opera, *Werther*, for which she has recently learned the role of Charlotte, and in French. Tebaldi said that she would enjoy singing Charlotte opposite the Werther of Franco Corelli, and she entertains hopes of at least recording that opera with him in the near future.

Another role that Tebaldi would like very much to sing is *Francesca da Rimini*, the opera composed by her early mentor

Riccardo Zandonai. She and Corelli recorded a long scene from *Francesca*'s third act as part of their recent recital disc for London-Decca. Tebaldi regrets a little that she hasn't sung the Verdi *Requiem* more frequently. This is one work which Renata also wishes she had recorded commercially.

Speaking of Tebaldi's records, when I asked her if she had a favorite she named three that she particularly liked: *La Traviata, Manon Lescaut*, and *La Gioconda*. She is also very pleased with the *Tebaldi Festival* set. She doesn't often listen to her own records, although she does study tapes of each performance that she gives in order to correct faults. The soprano has well-developed faculties of self-criticism, and, in discussing some of her own performances, it appeared that she can be very severe in her attitude toward her singing.

One evening, as I sat across from Tebaldi in her apartment concluding a lengthy interview, I was struck by some of the many apparent contradictions in her life. In defiance of time and nature, she appeared lovelier and younger with each year. An artist who has attained the highest pinnacles of her art, she studies each day, adding new detail to her roles and learning new music.

A woman who in many respects lives a very private life, she was generous with her time and pleased with the idea of a new book appearing about her. In spite of a great deal of publicity likening her to a madonna, or at least a saint, she has always been eager to admonish interviewers with "I am no saint!" I suspect that no one will ever truly know all there is to know about Renata Tebaldi. She is too used to bearing her sorrows alone, and, as an artist, has developed powers of introspection sufficiently great to enable her continually to reshape and rethink her approach to her work, so that her interpretations have grown over the years. Tebaldi surely deserves her privacy, as she has given so much of herself to her public throughout her career. She once stated that at each performance she leaves a piece of her heart on stage. Actually, she goes even further than that. She opens her soul, so to speak, making her characters live with her own feelings of love or pain. With her voice she has spread sunlight onto even the gloomiest of metaphorical skies, awakening with her song the pure joy of being alive and listening to such beautiful music. Like the diva of whom Cavarodossi sings in "Recondita armonia," Renata Tebaldi is the living embodiment of a wondrous harmony of colors, and in her singing, art and love will triumph forever.

Tebaldi in costume for Desdemona at the Metropolitan Opera (Melançon).

The Metropolitan Years

Renata's 1950 engagement at the San Francisco Opera, in which she made her American debut as Aïda, was not the prelude to an immediate engagement at the Metropolitan. Rudolf Bing, who had heard Tebaldi sing at a private party in Milan a year or two earlier, offered her a contract at the time of the California performances, but whether for reasons of repertoire (the debut role would have been Donna Elvira in *Don Giovanni*) or for other considerations, it was rejected, and five years were to pass before Tebaldi joined the New York company. In the meantime, Tebaldi scored several personal triumphs at La Scala, in Latin America, and elsewhere, and her recordings of complete operas began to fill the shops here. It became a clear case of "when," not "if," Renata would make her Metropolitan debut.

Francis Robinson, assistant manager of the Metropolitan and head of the Met's press department, recalled to me wistfully that while he had "fallen in love with Tebaldi" as soon as he heard her voice, he did not have the opportunity to meet her until she arrived in New York for her Metropolitan debut in January of 1955. Robinson remembers many a pleasant Sunday evening in Chicago when he and the soprano Edith Mason relaxed on the terrace of Mason's lakeside apartment, watching the sun set as Tebaldi's recordings were played on the phonograph. Ironically, on just such an occasion in 1950, Tebaldi passed through Chicago en route to San Francisco. Carrying a letter of introduction to Robinson from the Irish soprano Marguerite Sheridan, Tebaldi endeavored to reach the Metropolitan official, but through one of those hotel switchboard mixups that all travelers come to know and dread, the soprano's message was not delivered in time, and she left Chicago without having met him.

By the time of Tebaldi's debut at the Metropolitan, Rudolf Bing had reorganized that theatre; in 1954-55, he presided over a house that lengthened its season each year, steadily attracted new audiences, and commanded the services of most of the top singers of the day.

The 1954-55 season was Bing's fifth at the Met. His fiercest battles with the press and, more importantly, with company labor unions, still lay ahead, as did his tiff with Callas (she was not to make her Metropolitan debut until 1956, when she opened the season as Norma in Bellini's opera), and many of Bing's new products were of highest order. The season in which Tebaldi first appeared found such artists as Del Monaco, Warren, de los Angeles, Milanov, Stevens, London, Merrill, Peters, Albanese, Kirsten, Tucker, and Siepi prominent in the Italian and French repertoire. German opera was in its post-Flagstad-pre-Nilsson slump, while conductors included Stiedry, Monteux, Rudolph, and Cleva. Several weeks before Tebaldi's debut, Marian Anderson became the first black artist to sing at the Metropolitan, making her debut as Ulrica in *Un Ballo in Maschera*. New productions included *Andrea Chenier* and *Arabella*. Opening night that season, normally given over to the performance of one opera, was comprised of excerpts from *La Bohème, Il Barbiere di Siviglia* and *Aïda*, allowing such artists as Milanov, de los Angeles and Peters, not to mention Warren, Merrill, Bjoerling and Tucker, to share the stage. This bespoke the abundance of great singers on the roster, as well as the lack of ascendancy of any one particular soprano, tenor, or baritone. One element lacking from the company, however, was an authentic Italian (or italianate) lyric soprano of the highest order. Zinka Milanov, one of the century's great singers, was unquestionably the greatest Verdian soprano of her generation and, of course, a peerless exponent of many other Italian roles, but she was beginning her vocal decline in 1954. Furthermore, she was never associated to any great extent with such roles as Mimi, Manon Lescaut, and Butterfly. Victoria de los Angeles, whose exquisite taste and ethereal soprano voice made her one of the most beloved (and deservedly so) artists of Bing's first decade in New York, lacked ultimate warmth and power in Puccini operas, and she also busied herself with French and German repertoire. Kirsten and Albanese were undeniably Puccini specialists and distinguished artists as well, but neither lady had a voice that could truly be called great. Therefore, in the repertoire that she made her own, Tebaldi at her debut stood out like a beacon of light. In Francis Robinson's words, "she gave the entire company a lift."

The opera chosen for Renata's debut was *Otello,* and the date was January 31, 1955. Her Otello was Mario Del Monaco, with whom Renata had sung Aïda in San Francisco, and with whom she had already recorded several operas. Leonard Warren sang Iago, and the supporting cast included such artists as Martha Lipton as Emilia and Paul Franke as Cassio. The role of Roderigo was taken by James McCracken, who a few years later would become a leading dramatic tenor at the Met and elsewhere. (In fact, it was McCracken who sang Otello to Tebaldi's Desdemona in her most recent Metropolitan appearance.) Conducting the *Otello* was Fritz Stiedry.

Recalling the debut, the soprano noted that she felt joining the Met was one of the highest points of her career. Along with her La Scala debut, the New York debut was one of the two most important nights of her career. In spite of the magnitude of the event, and contrary to a "myth" that has arisen, the soprano clearly and firmly remembers that she felt no great nervousness that evening, and arrived at the opera house composed and ready to give her best work.

By all accounts, the evening was triumphant for all concerned, and Tebaldi was welcomed by public and critics alike. Writing in the *Herald Tribune,* Paul Henry Lang noted the five-year lag between Tebaldi's American and Metropolitan debuts: "it took another five years before New Yorkers could hear a voice that could rise above the din of the uproarious orchestra and sail on, pure and clear. But her pianissimos were just as audible in the big house, for they are not whispers, but beautifully rounded full-bodied tones. Needless to say, this style is in her bones and . . . she delivered her part with the traditional Italian sense for the vocal line. Miss Tebaldi is a noble artist and we are impatient to get better acquainted with her." Writing of the opera's final act, Lang declared that "it was here that Miss Tebaldi showed the full range of her talents. The 'Willow Song' was simplicity itself, but the asides between the verses trembled with terror, and the 'Ave Maria' was the last prayer, utterly moving and desperate, with its halting beginning, of a woman facing death."

Writing in the *World Telegram & Sun,* critic Louis Biancolli surrendered himself completely to Tebaldi, writing that "Miss Tebaldi would seem to have everything. The voice is full and firm and beautiful. It is capable of infinite shading and colored to suit every passing mood and fancy. The tones always lent glow and warmth to the gathering texture of Verdi's fabric of doom. At all times she handled the music with mastery, from the hushed, unearthly pianissimi of the love music and prayer to the stunned outcries of shame and terror. This Renata Tebaldi is a first-class musician and an artist of rare thoroughness." Virtually all the local reviewers echoed these sentiments, and, from all accounts, the ovations accorded Tebaldi at her early performances were as formidable as any in memory. The Metropolitan's national, unseen audience did not have to wait long to make the soprano's acquaintance, as her second performance was a Saturday matinee of *Otello* that was broadcast over the American Broadcasting Company network. It is difficult, of course, after long-standing familiarity with an artist, to imagine the impact of first hearing, but the millions in the Met's radio audience, sophisticates as well as novices, could hardly have failed to note the beauty and power of Tebaldi's singing, her exquisite phrasing, and her instinct for revealing the poetry and meaning behind each word and phrase.

In a repertory system that has since tended to give major artists maximum exposure in a minimum of roles each season, Tebaldi's repertoire during her first year at the Met is exciting for the opera buff to contemplate. In addition to *Otello,* she appeared in *La Bohème, Tosca* and *Andrea Chenier. Aïda* was also on her agenda but a throat ailment forced this performance to be postponed. So keen was the interest in Tebaldi's Aïda that, when she had to cancel, Rudolf Bing felt obliged to change the opera that evening, so that those who had ordered tickets especially to hear Tebaldi would not have to hear a replacement sing the role. This was a rare departure from policy, since tickets clearly state that casts are subject to change.

Mimi in *Bohème* was Tebaldi's second role at the Met. Reviewing the performance in the next morning's *New York Times,* Olin Downes found Tebaldi's Mimi "something of a revelation." Downes went on to say "For we have heard no Mimi who moved us so much by the sincerity and gripping emotion that she gave the part. One could even say that Miss Tebaldi, whose height is something that could easily be embarrassing to her partners on the stage, and whose stature gives her a more imposing effect than one naturally associates with . . . Mimi, makes the character in a manner proportionate to her height and a greater and more dramatic figure than one imagines [Mimi] to be."

Downes, of course, was neither the first nor the last to remark upon Tebaldi's special affinity for depicting Mimi, even though the soprano and the seamstress are of highly disparate physical types. Tebaldi herself is aware of this, although she herself can suggest no simple answer to the riddle, other than to say that Mimi is one role that she holds especially dear.

Others in the cast of Tebaldi's first Metropolitan *La Bohème* included Giuseppe Campora as Rodolfo, Ettore Bastianini as Marcello, Jean Fenn as Musetta, Norman Scott as Colline, and James McCracken (!) as Parpignol. Fausto Cleva, who was to work so closely with Tebaldi in years to come, conducted.

Tebaldi's first *Tosca* appearance at the Met was at a benefit for the Free Milk Fund for Babies, which used to sponsor an annual performance in order to raise money. Francis Robinson loves to recall the ritual "photo call" that went along with the benefit, at which the "lucky" prima donna had to pose smilingly with one of the infants who would share in the proceeds. Most years—and 1955 was no exception—the baby would cry and scream at his strange surroundings, and the unfamiliar "Mama" would gingerly attempt to cuddle it while flash bulbs popped in all directions. However, this time, the diva of the hour was Tebaldi. Robinson's eyes invariably light up as he describes how Tebaldi picked up the baby and began speaking to him gently in Italian. Almost immediately, it seems, he ceased his wailing as Tebaldi smiled down at him, and the photographers were able to proceed. Another story, less sentimental but equally delightful, is associated with this performance. Tebaldi, then making her first experiments with English, knew that this was a benefit performance for a children's organization. Somehow she thought at first that the children would attend the opera, as if it were a Guild student performance. Therefore Tebaldi confided to reporters that she felt sure the babies would enjoy *Tosca,* for it is very dramatic and exciting! Any initial chagrin she might have felt when her mistake was revealed to her ought to have been dissipated by the charmed smiles of those who heard her make it. Somehow one can't imagine a Callas or a Milanov ever letting her guard down enough to contribute such a moment of human comedy!

As for the performance itself, which took place on March 8, the reviewer for the *Times* told his readers that "The applause after 'Vissi d' arte' stopped the show for three minutes but the appeal of her singing in that aria was far from the only feature of the Italian soprano's impressive impersonation. Mme. Tebaldi's Tosca was emotionally vivid and individual, while faithful to the music and the drama. It carried dramatic expression throughout . . . As a whole, her impersonation must have been carefully studied and thought out, but it left an impression of spontaneity, of constant communication. It told of unified singing and significant action, and especially of the use of a wide range of vocal color and volume for musical and dramatic purposes achieved with striking success." The cast included Campora as Mario and Walter Casselas as Scarpia. Cleva conducted.

As noted, Tebaldi cancelled her *Aïda* on February 16, but she returned to the old opera house on 39th Street a week later for her first Metropolitan performance of Maddalena in *Andrea Chenier*. Giordano's opera had been revived at the beginning of the 1954-55 season for the first time in twenty-two seasons, with Mario Del Monaco in the title role, Leonard Warren as Gerard, Zinka Milanov as Maddalena, and the ubiquitous Maestro Cleva conducting. Given Milanov's preeminence in Italian dramatic soprano roles at the Metropolitan since 1938, the fans of both Tebaldi and Milanov must have been highly excited about Tebaldi's first appearance in *Chenier*. For, while there was no "reigning" Mimi, Tosca, or Desdemona at the Met at the time of Tebaldi's debut (Milanov had still to sing her first Metropolitan Tosca), Tebaldi was very definitely making designs on a territory that Zinka Milanov had carved out for herself. Of course, such rivalries are foolish and unnecessary, since there is always room for another great performance in an opera house, but the fact that the two ladies were "competing" as Maddalena must have lent a great deal of electricity to that first performance. By all accounts, the evening was memorable. Jay Harrison's highly perceptive review of the performance in the next day's edition of the *Tribune* discusses, seemingly for the first time in a New York publication, the question of the true nature of Tebaldi's voice, and the possible directions in which her career could go: "[Tebaldi] provided further fuel for the opposing Tebaldi factions that insist she must be either a dramatic soprano or a lyric one. Actually, however, she is neither and both. Her entire technique and training places her squarely in the middle of this dual category and thereby accounts at once for her every strength and weakness. The strength, as her Maddalena proclaimed, rests with a voice that can sing a ravishing pianissimo and still retain its glorious sweetness at even the loudest level. It is also highly flexible in its coloring and perfectly secure as it reaches for notes above the staff. In addition, Miss Tebaldi is an extraordinary musician who knows the value of every slight retardation and is not at all opposed to alter a tempo midway in a phrase if it suits the text's meaning and her own desires. And since she moves with uncommon grace and agility, her reading of Maddalena's role, combining extreme vocal refinement with theatrical plausibility, was all warmth and refinement." Harrison went on to note that Tebaldi's voice occasionally faltered momentarily as she shifted from lyrical singing to more passionate moments . . . an instance foreshadowing the soprano's future exploitation of the chest register for dramatic effect. Perhaps, if Renata Tebaldi was both a lyric and a dramatic soprano, as Harrison suggests, in the long run she might have been better off had she opted to remain a lyric one!

Other reviewers, although generally highly enthusiastic, also seemed to detect some elements of strain in Tebaldi's work that night (in a cast that included Del Monaco and Bastianini under Cleva's baton).

In retrospect, the role of Maddalena seems associated with Tebaldi both at her very best and in her most troubled vocal state. Her two commercial recordings of the role are successful, and reviewers who found her first Met Maddalena slightly blemished from a vocal standpoint almost apologized for quibbling! Tebaldi's 1960 Met broadcast of Maddalena reveals her to be still quite secure in the music with an easy command of smooth, glowing sound. Tebaldi's 1966 *Chenier* broadcast from the Met is notable for clarity of sound and dramatic impact, and the Sunday evening performance of the opera that preceded it stands out in my memory as quite the greatest performance of an Italian opera that I have ever attended. And yet, the nine Maddalenas that Tebaldi sang in New York in the fall of 1970 were perhaps the least successful series of appearances that she has ever made, as will be discussed later.

Maddalena, a figure in an opera more praised for its melodic inspiration and *brio* than for the intrinsic greatness of its music, is, like Tosca and Gioconda, a role that calls for attributes of lyric and dramatic sopranos, so that neither a true lyric nor a true dramatic voice can sing all of her music equally well. Theorists might say that, had Giordano been a greater composer, he would have seen to it that the tessitura lay more squarely within the range of one type of voice. However, even Verdi has been called a voice-wrecker, especially where such roles as Abigaille, Elena, and Violetta are concerned. Be that as it may, the role of Maddalena forces the singer to alternate frequently between quiet singing and loud, forceful vocalism. Even the healthiest of voices will suffer from prolonged exposure in this sort of role. Worst of all is that Maddalena, Gioconda, Tosca, and other such roles are among the most rewarding for the singer and the most popular with the public, so the temptation to meet their demands is overwhelming, and the immediate rewards for singing them equally heady. Yet virtually every major artist who alternated these roles with lyric parts suffered untimely vocal damage.

However, these problems still lay far ahead of Tebaldi as she concluded her first season at the Met. Her conquest of a great portion of the music-minded public was well under way, and the soprano had also begun to feel quite at home in New York. Tebaldi and her mother were not infrequently seen shopping for groceries in Little Italy, and a coterie of fans who survive to the present day lined the street outside the stage door of the Met before and (particularly) after each of her performances, knowing that it was Tebaldi's practice to sign the program of each and every fan who waited for that privilege. The Tebaldiani stopped traffic on West 40th Street on many a night!

Before rejoining the Metropolitan for the 1955-56 season, Tebaldi appeared once again with the San Francisco Opera, where her first Tosca so impressed the audience that she was obliged to encore "Vissi d'arte."

Tebaldi arrived in New York in time for her first Metropolitan *Aïda*, which took place on Saturday afternoon (regrettably, not broadcast) November 4. Moments before the opera began, Rudolf Bing posed with Tebaldi in her dressing room, commemorating the fact that she had signed a contract for the following spring (1957), at which time she would appear in a new production of *Traviata*. Since it was already public knowledge that Callas would make her debut on opening night of the next season, the rival fan clubs (as opposed to the divas themselves) could vie with each other—Callas's people gloated that their lady had the opening night, while the Tebaldi faction reminded them that Callas would appear in a seedy-looking production of *Norma* whereas Renata would have the Met's first new *Traviata* mise en scène in two decades built around her. At any rate, from the far leaner days of the 1970s, the Met in the mid-50s seemed to abound in great voices and larger-than-life personalities.

Tebaldi's Aïda on November 4, one of only three Met appearances in that opera, was ecstatically greeted by many. Howard Taubman in the *Times* found that "The Italian soprano has a mind and personality, and leaves her own impression on whatever role she undertakes. Her Aïda is only a slave when she has to be; unobserved, she is a princess of Ethiopia. Above all, she is a woman. When the messenger brings news in the first scene, this Aïda listens and reacts, she is not just a prima donna waiting her turn to sing. When her turn comes to sing, Miss Tebaldi does so with sovereign musicianship . . ." Cleva again conducted, and others in the cast included Mario Ortica making his Met debut as Radames, Blanche Thebom as Amneris, Bastianini as Amonasro, and Giorgio Tozzi as Ramfis. Although some in the audience felt that Aïda, like Maddalena, was a dangerously heavy role for Tebaldi, the immediate impact was that of one more solid success for her. More than one person who heard Tebaldi in those three Met Aïdas rank her ahead of even Milanov and Price in that role.

Tebaldi's Metropolitan appearances that season also included the roles of Maddalena in *Chenier* and Leonora in *La Forza del Destino*. The latter role, which Tebaldi also performed at La Scala in 1955, lay very well for the soprano's voice. In it, she demonstrated complete tonal security, as well as an aristocratic yet intense characterization. *Forza* was an opera that, until the 1950s, had been rather ill-served by the Met. Its local premiere wasn't until 1918, when Gatti-Casazza's Met presented Caruso and Rosa Ponselle (the latter making her

Metropolitan debut) in the leading roles. After Caruso's death, the opera languished and went unperformed for years at a time (there was a revival in the early 1940s) until Rudolf Bing gave the opera in a new and heavily cut production in 1952. This production has always been popular with Metropolitan audiences, and the 1956 performances, which matched Tebaldi with Tucker, Warren, Corena, and Hines, were sold out and, to judge from accounts of those present, memorable.

Tebaldi's next series of New York appearances was in the spring of 1957. The 1956-57 season may go down as the "Year of the Three Divas," during which Rudolf Bing struggled to allow Tebaldi, Callas, and Milanov equal places in the sun. Callas opened the season, but in a three-year-old production of Bellini's *Norma* originally designed for Mme. Milanov, the Met's reigning Norma since 1944. The stately Yugoslavian diva, who had herself been given two of Bing's first six opening nights, was placated by the invitation to sing Elvira in *Ernani,* in a new production that would be the Met's first performance of Verdi's fifth opera since the days of Ponselle. (It is interesting to reflect at this point that the operatic scene is so ruled by the cult of the soprano that, even though *Ernani* is dominated by three male roles—sung in this revival by Del Monaco, Warren, and Siepi, with a major conductor, Dimitri Mitropoulos—this production was known as Milanov's. Ironically, the soprano received some of the most severe criticism of her career for her singing in *Ernani.*)

However, if there was a local rivalry between Tebaldi and Zinka Milanov, it was as nothing compared to the furor fanned by the international press over the so-called Tebaldi-Callas feud. Recalling this now mythic "enmity," which gathered headlines around the free world for nearly two decades (and made Tebaldi and Callas household words for millions who never heard a note either lady ever sang), as well as the equally well-publicized "making-up" at Tebaldi's Metropolitan opening night in 1968, one is struck by the hollowness of the entire affair, and the lack of real incidents comprising it. The press—to the eventual benefit of both artists—bandied their names about at every conceivable opportunity. Although Tebaldi and Callas each delivered herself of a few stinging remarks about the other, the more sensational comments emanated, in reality, from overzealous press agents and gossip columnists.

The Great Feud, such as it was, began in Rio de Janeiro in the early 1950s. Callas and Tebaldi, friends from their early La Scala days, both graced a benefit concert one evening, along with a number of other visiting operatic luminaries. It had been agreed in advance, as a means of protecting overly sensitive egos, that no one would sing an encore. Unfortunately, democracy works as unevenly in South American opera houses as in the South American parliaments. Tebaldi's Rio appearances had been highly successful that year, while Callas had not been in top form. At any rate, Callas, who preceded Tebaldi in the concert, received but respectful applause, while Tebaldi was treated to a full-scale ovation. In what was probably intended as a gracious gesture to the friendly public, Tebaldi sang an encore. In retrospect, this was perhaps an unwise move, and possibly Callas had a right to be miffed. However, this is not the sort of thing about which people go to war—unless they are opera stars. Being opera stars, the two sopranos squared off and fought the most senseless battle since Lenski and Eugene Onegin shot it out in the second act of Tchaikovsky's opera.

Callas stopped speaking to Tebaldi. She did, however, speak, through her press agents, about her. Within weeks, each of the disputing parties had assumed a posture that she would maintain throughout the decade and a half that followed. Callas usually appeared as the aggressor, making tempestuous comments to reporters, including the celebrated and very silly remark to the effect that to compare Callas to Tebaldi would be like comparing champagne to coca-cola. Tebaldi tended to remain regally silent, in the manner of one of Verdi's long-suffering heroines, although at one point she was sufficiently irked to send a letter to *Time*, in whose pages Callas had disparaged her voice. "I may not have a voice like Mme. Callas," wrote an uncharacteristically self-deprecating Tebaldi, "but I do have one important thing that Mme. Callas has not: a heart!"

Then, of course, there was the incident at La Scala in which Tebaldi sang *Aïda* and Callas turned up in the audience, sitting in a box. During the Nile scene, that night, there was a disturbance in the Callas box . . . it seemed that Callas had lost a piece of jewelry and was searching for it with the aid of an usher while Tebaldi was singing "O patria mia."

Actually, the whole idea of a Callas-Tebaldi feud seems juvenile and foolish, especially since the entire affair was based on such ridiculous incidents as those just described. To the credit of both artists, each claims today that there was never much of a feud to begin with. When I broached the subject to Tebaldi in June of 1973, she smiled and again denied any real enmity between her and Callas, to whom she always refers to as "Maria." As Tebaldi put it: "First, Maria would say something to the press, then I would have to say something. Then, Maria would say something else, so I would have to answer with something new."

Tebaldi also notes that, whatever the cost to either "rival" in terms of nervous energy, the so-called feud had many practical benefits: "After all, it brought both Maria and me a great deal of publicity. She sold many recordings and so did I!"

If Tebaldi and Callas themselves never paid much attention to the war between their press representatives, the same cannot be said for their fans. Callas fans demonstrated at Tebaldi performances at La Scala, and those who booed Callas at her appearances were often said to be "Tebaldiani."

During the 1955 season at the Chicago Lyric Opera, much was made of the fact that both Tebaldi and Callas were on the roster, occasionally appearing within a night of each other. One would have thought that the city of Chicago was not big enough to accommodate both divas!

Actually, the most interesting aspect of the feud is that one must agree with Callas's statement that she and Tebaldi were not rivals. Although Callas's remark was shortly expanded to belittle Tebaldi's choice of repertoire, the truth is that the only roles they shared to any great extent were Violetta in *La*

Traviata and the title role in *Tosca*. True, both sopranos sang Aïda, Maddalena in *Chenier*, and Fedora, but much of Callas's greatness lay in her Bellini and Donizetti heroines, while Tebaldi will be remembered as peerless in the Puccini operas, other *verismo* roles, and in such Verdian roles as Desdemona, Leonora in *Forza*, and Mistress Alice Ford in *Falstaff*. In truth, for most of their careers, the two sopranos' repertoires were as different as, say, Tebaldi's and Joan Sutherland's—even granting that Sutherland is a wonderful Violetta and, in her early career, sang Desdemona, Tosca, and Eva in *Meistersinger*. Considerable space is devoted to Tebaldi versus Callas in the chapter "Tebaldi the Artist," so it suffices to end this digression by paraphrasing Callas's "champagne" remark: to compare the two sopranos would be like comparing champagne to Chivas Regal—both are superb and a choice of one over the other would be fruitless!

To return to the 1956-57 Met season, Callas' opening night *Norma* was received with reservations by critics, as was the Elvira sung by Milanov a few weeks later.

Tebaldi arrived in mid-winter to prepare for the *Traviata*. Bing had engaged some of the most impressive theatrical talent available to insure that the Metropolitan's first new *Traviata* in more than two decades would be a memorable revival. Oliver Smith, who had designed numerous Broadway plays and musicals, including *My Fair Lady*, created the settings, while Rolf Gerard, one of Bing's favorite scenic artists, was retained for the costuming. The stage director was the late Sir Tyrone Guthrie, while Tebaldi's musical colleagues included conductor Fausto Cleva, Giuseppe Camporas as Alfredo, and Leonard Warren as the elder Germont.

This *Traviata* was Tebaldi's first new production at the Metropolitan, which in practical terms, meant that it was the first time in her Met career that she would wear costumes designed with her in mind, and, most importantly, take part in blocking rehearsals, at which the physical movements of the characters were plotted and dramatic interpretations evolved.

Stage direction proved the major stumbling block during the rehearsal period. Tyrone Guthrie was an experienced and often brilliant man of the theatre. He brought to the production his own ideas of characterization as well as the determination to have his principal artists act as well as sing. But he failed to take into consideration the reluctance of many singers to engage in much action while singing. Furthermore, Tebaldi had sung Violetta before, including appearances in a slightly controversial production at La Scala; although acclaimed on musical grounds, the performance had inspired some reservations about her characterization of Violetta. The criticism, however, was relatively mild, and presumably Tebaldi had no reason to doubt her ability to give her audiences a Violetta that ranked with the finest of her other roles.

Part of the problem was that the Metropolitan needed a new *Traviata* at precisely the time when Tebaldi was due for a new production. Even the fact that her voice was on the heavy side for Act One could not interfere with this marriage between the company's needs and its desire to provide a major artist with a "plum." Therefore, it was probably inevitable that the rehearsals went less smoothly than Rudolf Bing had envisioned. Tebaldi continually questioned the staging she was being called upon to perform, and, it appears, resisted Guthrie's efforts to alter substantially her conception of Violetta Valery.

In addition, Tebaldi was unsure about the attractiveness of the costumes designed for her by Gerard. In particular, she remembers being distressed by the yellow summer dress she was supposed to wear in the second act, which is set in the country villa shared by Violetta and Alfredo. "I really did not like the dress, and at one rehearsal when Mr. Bing was there, I went to him and told him this. Mr. Bing told me that he thought the dress was lovely, and promised that during the next rehearsal break, he would have someone model the dress onstage for me under the lights, so that I myself would see that it was a nice costume. So, a little later, when we stopped work, I was invited to sit down in the auditorium, and sure enough a model walked out onto the stage wearing my dress and sunhat from that scene . . . but the model was Mr. Bing! Of course I laughed and laughed, but I had to admit that Bing was right about that dress!" Bing's jest, whether improvised in a moment of mischief, or more carefully calculated, served to alleviate the tensions building up during these rehearsals.

Whatever Tebaldi's reservations about her costumes, they were nothing in comparison to her distaste for Guthrie's staging. Renata brought to *Traviata* a conception that had been hers for nearly a decade, as well as the experience of successful productions in Italy and Latin America. Not surprisingly, she resented Guthrie's efforts to radically change her performance. From her point of view, Tebaldi was justified in her annoyance, for was not this *Traviata* her own vehicle?

In the long run, Tebaldi's notions as to the proper manner of performing Violetta won. Her views were borne out by the response to the opera, for she scored a major success with critics and public alike when the production premiered in February 1957.

Even with reservations concerning her singing of "Sempre libera," Tebaldi received a number of enthusiastic notices for her Met Violetta. Lang, in the *Tribune*, wrote that "Miss Tebaldi threw herself into her role with her customary ardor, and her superb vocal resources shone in all their splendor, perhaps a bit too much so in the first act. It was moving to watch her as she was invaded by feelings heretofore unknown to her, but believing herself marked for life because of her past, she tears herself away from these tender thoughts. The mood is expressed in brilliant coloraturas, flexible and beautifully projected."

In the *New York Times*, Howard Taubman admired Tebaldi's singing, although he was more bothered than Lang by that first act: "Miss Tebaldi is a Violetta in the grand line . . . Miss Tebaldi's voice, for all its quality and control, is not quite comfortable in the tessitura of 'Sempre libera' as written." Taubman then noted the downward transposition, going on to say, in part, that "instead of having to soar to D flat, Miss Tebaldi had only to reach B natural, which she did resplendently. One is willing to forgive this adjustment in the face of Miss Tebaldi's art. Her voice is in its fairest form this season. It pours out with plenitude and purity in the big moments, and it has irresistible delicacy and poignancy in the subdued passages. Her singing throughout is musical, immersed in the emotions of the character. If the 'Sempre libera' has not the last word in brilliance, it remains flexible and vibrant. She spun out a *pianissimo* of gossamer fineness in the 'Dite alla giovane.' Aside from several moments of being off-pitch, she sang gloriously."

Louis Biancolli, one of Tebaldi's most vociferous admirers among the gentlemen of the press, also found her Violetta slightly flawed but very satisfying. In the *World Telegram & Sun,* he wrote: "there was again that magnificent gush of tone to make one overlook the liberties of tempo and dynamics. This was a Violetta irresistible to the eye, ear, and heart. It was a Violetta that, to be sure, applied some excess weight to the lyric line of the early passages. [After the first act] Madame Tebaldi was compelling in every sense, rising steadily to the season's summit of drama, intensity and voice. . . . This was a gorgeously gowned and regal Violetta, by no stretch of the imagination on the Sick List, but a Violetta who through glowing power of voice, grace of gesture and deep expressiveness reached and touched the heart."

Tebaldi's Violetta was an honest, tender, and passionate creature. Once past the pyrotechnical hurdles of the first act, the soprano conveyed all the power and beauty of Verdi's music. The subtle build-up of dramatic tension in the scene with Germont was impressive, and the explosively dramatic quality of the "Ah, m'ami Alfredo" provided the catharsis that Verdi surely intended. Equally appealing was the sadness of the soprano's "Alfredo, Alfredo" in the third act finale, while the handling of the letter-reading and the "Addio del passato" was all that one could have wished for. The entire performance, though, might have been aided by more relaxed, freely flowing tempi than those chosen by Fausto Cleva.

Tebaldi's 1957-58 season at the Metropolitan never, in fact, took place, for on the evening she was scheduled to make her first appearance, her mother suffered a heart attack. Signora Giuseppina Tebaldi, who had been the soprano's inseparable companion throughout her career, died just over a week later, on Saturday morning, November 30, 1957. Tebaldi was scheduled to sing the role of Aïda at that day's matinee, to be broadcast coast-to-coast. Throughout the week-long death vigil at the Tebaldi apartment in the Hotel Buckingham, Tebaldi had hardly moved out of her mother's presence. As the dying woman seemed to rally slightly the day before the broadcast, Tebaldi considered singing if her mother's condition continued to improve. However, Signora Tebaldi took a turn for the worse and died, leaving her daughter inconsolable. The day was doubly sad for opera lovers, for, in addition to the news of Tebaldi's loss, word came from Italy that the great tenor Beniamino Gigli had died the same day. Francis Robinson recalls, with a sense of life's irony, that on December 1 he had first to pay a sympathy visit to Tebaldi and then to go on to New York Hospital, where he congratulated Senator John Kennedy upon the birth of his daughter Caroline.

So much has been written about the special bond between Renata Tebaldi and her mother that it suffices to note here that Renata considered her mother the greatest, and virtually her only, outside source of emotional strength. Although she had initially opposed her daughter's switch from the study of piano to that of voice, once she became convinced of her potential as a singer, she sacrificed her entire life for Tebaldi's career. Her life as a none-too-wealthy woman separated from her husband in a small Italian town had been less than perfectly comfortable; but to taking up the burdens of international travel and the frenetic pace of the operatic scene, at the same time making hotel rooms in foreign cities throughout Europe and the Americas seem as homelike as possible, required a great deal of physical and emotional strength. The bond of love that united Renata Tebaldi and her mother really defies description. Speaking of her mother in the summer of 1973, Tebaldi takes on a far-away expression, and her eyes still brim with tears.

Vehemently rejecting, as she always has, any suggestion that her relationship with her mother was perhaps too close for her own good, Tebaldi stresses that it was only love that brought them so close, and that she never felt restricted or even overprotected by her mother's presence.

Given their closeness, it is not surprising that Tebaldi mourned her mother deeply, and felt compelled to cancel all appearances for several months. Indeed, she has said since that in those dark days shortly after her mother's death she seriously considered giving up her career. But she was dissuaded from this by her friends, who reminded her of her mother's many sacrifices, which made her early career possible, as well as her great pleasure in her daughter's successes. However, it was not until spring of 1958 that Tebaldi felt able to resume her career. The occasion was a production of *Madama Butterfly* in Barcelona that marked the soprano's first stage appearances as Cio-cio-san.

Renata spent the summer of 1958 making recordings, including the stereophonic remakes of *Madama Butterfly* and *Tosca,* and returned to New York in October to open the 1958-59 Metropolitan season as Tosca. She had not sung in the United States since early November of the previous year, when she appeared in Chicago in the title role of *Adriana Lecouvreur,* only a few weeks before the death of her mother. December 22, 1958 was the hundredth anniversary of the birth of Giacomo Puccini, and the Metropolitan was preparing to celebrate this event by including all four of the Puccini operas then in its active repertoire—*Manon Lescaut, La Bohème, Tosca,* and *Madama Butterfly*—in its schedule that season. (*Turandot* and *La fanciulla del West,* both of which were successfully revived in the following decade, were, one assumes, still thought to be unsafe at the box office!) Tebaldi was invited to sing the heroines of all four Puccini works. This meant that, in addition to the honor of being chosen to sing on a Met opening night, she was also to sing the roles of Manon Lescaut and Cio-cio-san for the first time in her Metropolitan career. Tebaldi's importance to the Met was further demonstrated early that season when Callas and Bing could not reach an agreement concerning that lady's performance schedule, with the result that Bing most unceremoniously—and unfairly—dropped Callas from the Met.

Even without the firing of Callas, Tebaldi's local return would have been greeted with excitement. *Tosca* has always been extremely popular in New York, seldom absent from the repertoire for more than a season at a time. Since it was not being given a new production, it was hardly a novelty for a Metropolitan First Night. However, Tebaldi and co-stars Del Monaco (Mario Cavaradossi) and George London (Scarpia), as well as conductor Mitroupoulos, were sufficient box-office lures to sell the house out well in advance, with inflated prices bringing the Met a take of something over $86,000 for the performance.

The critical reaction was generally enthusiastic. Miles Kastendiek, writing in the *Journal-American,* found that "Tebaldi and Del Monaco strove to sing as they never did before. The result was inartistic[!] but provocative of vocal decibels guaranteed to win them cheers and bravos galore." It seems that some critics will never accept passionate *verismo* singing as artistic.

Paul Henry Lang, reviewing that opening night *Tosca* for the *Herald-Tribune,* seemed heartily impressed with what he heard, although he found certain moments slightly disturbing: "It was good to have Miss Tebaldi back at the Met, for she represents the supreme good in opera: singing with a beautiful voice. It seems to me that this great artist has gained in the intensity of her delivery and in her ability to correlate musical with dramatic values. When she faced Scarpia, there was murder in her voice, a hatred and desperation more real in sound than when she stabbed her tormentor physically. Her voice is still admirably pliable in the *pianos* and soars free in the climactic scenes, causing wild demonstrations and frenetic applause. I say 'still' because it seems to me that Miss Tebaldi is too prodigal with her great gifts; there are signs indicating that she is singing too much. And the novel tones someone taught her to use for dramatic effect are not becoming to a high soprano. But, Tebaldi is Tebaldi, and we are thankful to her."

Thus, in 1958, the sensitive Mr. Lang realized that Tebaldi was facing several problems that would cause her a good deal of trouble years later. One was largely a matter of taste: the tendency to overuse the chest register would from time to time mar later performances. The idea that Tebaldi was being "too prodigal with her great gifts" was perhaps truer than either would have guessed. One of the most striking factors of Tebaldi's artistry has always been that she gives all she has to give at each performance. She never seems to be holding back, nor is there ever a sense of technique or artifice replacing real voice. One of the reasons for the genuine excitement of a Tebaldi performance is this awareness that nothing is ever being withheld; yet, in retrospect, it seems likely that the singer gave too much of her voice at each performance. When it became less physically easy for her to produce the amplitude of sound to which she, and her audiences, had grown accustomed, Renata began to force, seemingly to push conciously for bigger sound, rather than scaling effects down. This would perhaps have been more practical but, to Tebaldi's way of thinking, less artistically honest. This matter of singing with "capital" instead of with "interest," as some singers put it, has brought more than a few artists to grief. Given the vocal resources that were Renata Tebaldi's at the outset of her career, it is understandable that she, like countless numbers who heard her, began to believe she could achieve virtually anything she wanted with them.

In the 1970's, when Renata could no longer equal her own work of a decade or longer earlier, her singing was always on a grand, even heroic scale. Even if a high C was achieved only with painful effort and the note was more exciting than truly beautiful, the listener always felt that the "sense" of the music was present, that Tebaldi had not cheated by omitting the note entirely. It was as if she were phrasing and projecting the music as she had done in earlier days, but the physical apparatus for producing the notes to some degree had worn away. This sincerity and honesty of performing made Tebaldi still a great singer after her finest evenings in the opera house were behind her.

The fact remains that the 1958-59 Metropolitan season was one of Tebaldi's most successful engagements at any theatre. Just a few weeks after the gala *Tosca* performance, she sang her first Cio-cio-san with the Met. The previous spring Rudolf Bing had revived *Butterfly* in a new production designed by

Motohiro Nagasaka and staged by Yoshio Aoyama. These two men, prominent in Tokyo theatrical productions, produced in their collaboration a handsome mise en scène filled with realistic details of architecture and strikingly beautiful Japanese costumes, as well as a staging that lent credibility to the gestures and physical appearance of the Oriental characters.

The production, still in use today, was a great success at the time. Since the transformation of the production's first Butterfly, Antonietta Stella, from an Italian prima donna into a "real" Japanese maiden had aroused much favorable comment, Big retained director Aoyama, to rehearse several other singers who would assume the role the following season. Therefore Tebaldi had the opportunity to work with Aoyama. Despite her height, she managed to create, from all accounts, the illusion of fragility and related "Japanese" qualities necessary for Cio-cio-san. If her appearance was Japanese, Tebaldi's sound was as opulent and "Italian" as ever, and the reviews were ecstatic.

Jay Harrison's review of the first performance, which took place on November, seems euphoric: "Renata Tebaldi, singing the title role in *Madama Butterfly* for the first time at the Metropolitan Opera Saturday night, gave what is likely to go down as a historic performance . . . what is even more unusual, however, is the fact that Tebaldi at first glance does not seem to be the Butterfly type at all . . . The impression she gave was that of a soprano very much in love with a role that she was singing for every shred of its italianate power and glory. The Japanese illusion was secondary, though Miss Tebaldi was marvelously made up and has learned to accommodate all of the mincing gestures, deep bows, and fluttering movements that are standard equipment for the part. But it was her voice that sold the character and made it movingly real. I do not recall offhand a Butterfly as musically sung, as elegantly phrased. Miss Tebaldi seized every opportunity to mould, curve and arch her lines; there was not an instant in which she failed to find vocal colors appropriate to the needs of the text. That is how great characterizations are made. That is how Miss Tebaldi made her Butterfly."

Strangely, Tebaldi never sang *Madama Butterfly* on a broadcast performance, so, the nation as a whole never had an opportunity to hear her in a live performance. Nor do there seem to be any surviving tapes of her Metropolitan Cio-cio-sans.

Tebaldi's other "new" role that season, Puccini's *Manon Lescaut, was* broadcast, several weeks after its premiere on December 3. Richard Tucker sang Des Grieux, Frank Guarrera was Lescaut, Ezio Flagello was Geronte, and Cleva conducted. According to sources present at the first performance, Cleva's conducting was listless enough to prevent the score from igniting, but the singing of Tebaldi and Tucker was acclaimed and the entire opera did indeed come to life on the broadcast performance. Interestingly, Tebaldi's final *Manon Lescaut* of the season, scheduled for January 23, was cancelled by the management when Tebaldi informed them that she could not perform owing to an infected throat. As with the cancelled *Aïda* four years earlier, Rudolf Bing felt that enough people in the audience had purchased tickets specifically to hear Tebaldi to warrant changing the bill (to *Tosca*), and allowing refunds. According to Irving Kolodin's history of the Metropolitan Opera, Bing lost 11,000 additional dollars that night as a result. The cancellation deprived Metropolitan subscribers of another chance to hear Tebaldi at the very pinnacle of her career in one of her most successful roles. Rarely did Tebaldi seem as passionately involved in her characterization as she was in Puccini's Manon, and even if there were a few tell-tale signs of future vocal problems that season, they were hardly in evidence in *Manon Lescaut.* There was an element of voluptuousness in her Manon, particularly in the second act, that has been unsurpassed in anything else I have heard Tebaldi do.

Tebaldi's one non-Puccini role that season was Desdemona in *Otello.* A tape of the broadcast performance, in which she was flanked by Del Monaco and Warren, with Cleva conducting, reveals these three singers in even more secure form than at the broadcast of February, 1955. The clarity of Tebaldi's sound that day was absolute and her histrionic intensity staggering. She has recorded the role of Desdemona commercially twice, and there are dozens of tapes of other Tebaldi Desdemonas, but none is surpassed by this performance.

Fifteen years of perspective show the 1958-59 season as Tebaldi's greatest at the Met. She was a secure, "reigning" diva then, in full command of her voice and ever increasing her power as an actress. After that season, her appearances were clouded from time to time by tragedy (as in Warren's death the following year), her own illness, and the inescapable fact that by the late 1960s her voice, however much beauty, strength, and power remained, was not the seemingly invincible instrument it had been ten years earlier.

The 1959-60 Met season was a shorter than usual one for Tebaldi, who was scheduled to return to the company in February to prepare for the role of Amelia Grimaldi in Verdi's *Simon Boccanegra.* This opera was being revived by the Metropolitan for the first time in twelve years, in a new production with Leonard Warren as Simon, Richard Tucker as Gabriele Adorno, Giorgio Tozzi as Fiesco, Ezio Flagello as Paolo, and Dimitri Mitropoulos conducting. The noted director Margaret Webster, who had staged the *Don Carlo* production that opened the Bing regime, was taking charge of the drama. Unfortunately, an attack of the flu forced Tebaldi to remain in Italy several additional weeks, so that she was unable to sing Amelia at either the dress rehearsal or the first few performances. Her place was taken by Mary Curtis-Verna, the versatile American "house soprano" who had replaced her in *Aïda* on the day of her mother's death. Tebaldi had arrived in New York the week of the premiere of *Boccanegra,* but did not wish to perform the role without adequate rehearsal.

Thus, Tebaldi's first appearance in New York that season was rescheduled for March 4, three nights after the first *Boccanegra.* The opera was *La Forza del Destino* with Messrs. Warren and Tucker, as well as Jerome Hines and Salvatore Baccaloni, joining her. Thomas Schippers conducted. What made that evening unforgettable was in no way connected with the singing, as estimable as that may have been; the performance was terminated midway in the second act when Leonard Warren collapsed and died as he was about to conclude Don Carlo di Vargas's *cabaletta.* One can well imagine that Warren's on-stage colleagues were as thunderstruck as the audience when they saw the powerful baritone fall "like a column" to the floor without so much as a cry for help. Richard Tucker, watching his friend Warren from the wings along with Rudolf Bing, witnessed the gruesome scene, but Tebaldi was off in her dressing room when Warren fell dying to the floor. Bing assured the audience that the performance would continue; when Warren was pronounced dead, however, the general manager was compelled to cancel it. As the ladies' dressing rooms were on the opposite side of the house from the men's in the old Met, it is quite possible, as Francis Robinson recollects, that Tebaldi left the theatre without knowing that Warren had actually died. However, such news travels like lightning in a theatre, and performances are not cancelled or cut short lightly (indeed, this was the first such instance at the Met in this century), It is more likely that Tebaldi sensed, even if no one wished to tell her, that Warren had died. Warren was not a particularly close friend of Tebaldi's, but her Met career had brought the two artists together in New York and on tour many times. He had, of course, sung Iago to her Desdemona on the night of her debut, nearly five years earlier, and had sung with her as well in *Tosca, Chenier,* and *Forza.* Warren had many of Tebaldi's own attributes: a huge, sensuously beautiful voice, extraordinary musicianship, and a stately yet galvanizing stage presence. Judging from tape recordings of their performances, Warren and Tebaldi worked well together, and it is unfortunate that they never recorded together on a commercial label. Warren's death on the first night of Renata's American season in 1960 must have shaken her tremendously. Interestingly, although she sang several more complete *Forzas* that year including the broadcast performance the following Saturday in which Warren's place was taken by Mario Sereni, she never sang Lenora again after that season.

Later in the season Tebaldi sang Amelia to the Simon Boccanegra of Frank Guarrera, and Maddalena in *Andrea Chenier,* which she sang on a memorable broadcast in late March, with Tucker in the title role. That afternoon found Tebaldi in prime condition to take up the challenges of the Giordano heroine, singing with a particular brightness of sound; if there was metal in her high notes, it was gold rather than steel.

Warren's death caused a frantic search for substitute baritones to replace him in performances for which the dead giant had been scheduled. It is interesting to note that Tebaldi thus sang a *Tosca* with Hermann Uhde as Scarpia. Uhde, who himself died tragically young a few years later, was a major interpreter of Wagnerian and other German roles, and had scored a triumph as Berg's Wozzeck a few weeks earlier in the Met's belated premiere of that opera.

Another baritone with whom Renata sang in New York that season was Anselmo Colzani, who made his debut as Simon Boccanegra on April 7. Colzani was a jovial Bolognese with a highly serviceable voice and a strong talent for acting. He often shared the stage with Tebaldi in such operas as *Tosca, Chenier, La fanciulla del West, Otello* and *Gioconda*, as well as *Boccanegra*.

The 1960-61 season was neither Tebaldi's longest nor her most exciting, as she added no new roles to her local list, nor were any new productions created for her; her appearances included such "usual" roles as Cio-cio-san and Amelia Grimaldi.

Amelia is one of the few Verdi heroines who are musically subservient to the baritone and bass, and dramatically staid as well. Still, she does have a lovely aria and a brilliant duet with Boccanegra, and a pleasant if less inspired scene with the tenor, and Tebaldi made the most of her material, singing a heroine of considerable taste and charm.

I am sure that Tebaldi would agree with me that her greatest triumph at the Met in 1960-61 was offstage—namely Rudolf Bing's consent to one of Tebaldi's pet projects; a revival, scheduled for the following season of Francesco Cilea's opera *Adriana Lecouvreur*. Cilea was one of Tebaldi's earliest admirers, and he told her on more than one occasion that she would be perfect as the heroine of his one opera that achieved any sort of international reputation. Indeed, the role lay well for her voice, its music is syrupy but attractive, and Tebaldi had sung it in Italy and Chicago with much success. Not surprisingly, she was eager to add Adriana to her Metropolitan roles. Bing, who confessed to me years later that he despised the opera, had other considerations besides his own taste to mull over. *Adriana* hadn't been performed at the Met since the turn of the century, when Caruso and Lina Cavalleri sang it; thus it would require new production, which, given the eighteenth-century French setting, would need to be lavish and therefore expensive. Then too, a star tenor and mezzo-soprano would be needed to support the soprano lead. Nonetheless general managers, even those with great authority and reputation for toughness, cannot afford to alienate too many of their leading singers, and eventually Sir Rudolf came around. Tebaldi, who until 1961 had had to content herself with singing Adriana's "signature" aria, "Io son l'umile ancella," at the 1958 New Year's Eve gala sequence in *Die Fledermaus,* recalls that when Bing telephoned her one day and asked if she would like to sing *Adriana* the next season, she was so surprised and delighted that she fell into a chair from shock.

Bing, shrewd manager that he was, had waited to revive Adriana until he had found a tenor able to partner Tebaldi in the role of Maurizio. Franco Corelli, who had made his debut in January 1961 as Manrico in *Trovatore,* was with his good looks and clarion voice, an ideal choice. The production was to be a duplicate of a very beautiful Rome Opera production, with new costumes designed for Tebaldi. Thus the soprano left New York with a contract in her pocket and triumph in her eyes, and went on to make a spectacular reappearance at La Scala as Tosca after an absence of several seasons. The La Scala *Tosca* also featured Giuseppe di Stefano as Mario, yet it is safe to say that virtually all eyes and ears were focused on Tebaldi, whose entrance was hailed with ecstatic shouts from the crowd and whose path was strewn with flowers as she returned to her car after her performance.

All but mobbed by well-wishers as she and her entourage drove through Milan, Tebaldi enjoyed a truly spectacular homecoming.

However, amidst all these happy events, forces beyond the control of Tebaldi, Bing, or any other individual were moving to create difficulties that would keep the soprano away from the United States for nearly two years.

Rudolf Bing was never noted for tact or soft-heartedness when it came to dealing with labor unions. Thus informed opera fans were shocked but not entirely surprised when the Met's orchestra called a strike several weeks before the 1961-62 season was to begin. As negotiations became deadlocked, Bing announced that the season would be cancelled. At that point, President Kennedy sent Secretary of Labor Arthur Goldberg to New York to participate in negotiations, and Goldberg was successful in bringing the musicians and the Metropolitan's management to terms.

Along with the general rejoicing came word from Bing that in the month before the settlement, when the season had been in doubt, a number of projects had been cancelled, or at least postponed. Among them was *Adriana Lecouvreur*. When this news reached Tebaldi in Europe, her reaction was to cancel what remained of her Metropolitan commitments for the coming season. This tactic did not move Bing to reconsider, although the soprano was assured that *Adriana* would be mounted for her the following year. In addition, Bing offered her an unprecedented second new production for the 1962-63 season, Verdi's *Otello,* with James McCracken and Robert Merrill as her leading men. Tebaldi accepted these offers, but her decision not to appear in New York until *Adriana* was to be performed remained final.

One of Tebaldi's major European engagements that season was a revival of Giordano's *Fedora* in Naples, in which, under the baton of Arturo Basile, she was flanked by Giuseppe di Stefano and Mario Sereni. The performance revealed some disturbing signs that were to become still more evident a year or so later. Particularly in the first act, Tebaldi's voice sounded very heavy and was produced with far less ease than before. In the second and third acts, things improve considerably for

Tebaldi, who seemed nearer her usual stride. Still, she eschewed an optional high C in the second act duet with Loris (di Stefano), and even in the third act, which moved extraordinarily well dramatically as well as musically, the listener had a definite feeling that something was wrong.

Between *Fedoras* and the *Adriana* premiere at the Met, Tebaldi suffered a painful inflammation of one leg that required her to be immobile and her leg encased in a cast for several months, a situation that did nothing for her nerves. Following her recovery, she embarked on a strenuous reducing diet. Though always a handsome woman, prior to 1963 she was not especially glamorous. Her clothes were always chosen with great care and taste, and the general effect of her appearance was one of imposing elegance, but the fact remained that Tebaldi felt she would look better if she were slimmer.

Since physical heft is considered by many to be essential for the production and preservation of a great operatic voice, most singers look askance at sudden weight losses, fearing the equally sudden loss of the voice as well. Maria Callas lost more than a hundred pounds between 1953 and 1955, and her voice began to develop really serious problems after she slimmed down. Although it can be argued that her choice of roles also contributed to the tragically early deterioration of her instrument.) In any case Tebaldi was determined to show New Yorkers a more glamorous figure upon her return to the Met's stage, and she dieted away some forty pounds by early 1963.

Tebaldi arrived in New York in early January 1963 to take part in rehearsals for *Adriana*. If she felt at all tired or otherwise unwell, she said nothing to those around her and threw herself into the work at hand. Reporters and magazine writers had a field day photographing the "new" Tebaldi, who now displayed a youthful figure, chic clothes, and the Titian red hair that she has worn ever since. Local journalists were hampered by the fact that there was a newspaper strike going on in New York City, but the singer was treated to her second feature story in *Time* magazine, and other publications commented upon her new style of dress.

Adriana had its premiere on January 21. First-nighters, if dazzled by Renata's physical radiance, were shocked by the fact that her singing was not up to snuff. According to those present, she sounded tired and the voice was heavier than ever before; this was a dull, strained sort of heaviness, as opposed to the free-flowing power of her singing on virtually all other occasions. High notes were edgy and occasionally off-pitch. Evidently the second performance was not a great deal better. I myself attended the third performance, which coincided with the soprano's birthday, February 1. On this occasion, things seemed to go better. Not too much strain was evident, and the audience seemed pleased. Tebaldi received one of the longest ovations I have ever witnessed following the final act. She did indeed look ravishing, and appeared relaxed and content, seemingly enjoying the reception she was receiving. The matinee broadcast performance, which followed a week later, also went fairly well. The voice did lack some of its former opulence but, from the viewpoint of a decade or more later, Tebaldi's singing during this grave vocal "crisis" seems inferior only when judged by her former standard of performance.

Whatever the fans—or, for that matter, the critics—thought, Tebaldi herself was very alarmed by her vocal state; after the broadcast performance, she felt compelled to cancel not only the remaining *Adriana* appearances but the rest of her American season as well, including the new *Otello.* The role of Desdemona eventually went to Gabriella Tucci, a charming and distinguished artist in her own right, while Licia Albanese and Mary Curtis-Verna shared the Cilea heroine for the remainder of the season.

And thus Renata Tebaldi, for the first time in a career spanning two decades, tasted something less than success if not outright failure. In addition, critical opinion was against *Adriana Lecouvreur* as an opera relevant to 1963. It was unpleasant to contemplate that Tebaldi's least successful Met appearances were in what she considered her favorite role. The production itself, though, was quite handsome and decently staged, except for a truly awful setting of the third act ballet on the theme of the Judgment of Paris. Corelli scored a major success as Maurizio, and Irene Dalis and Colzani did well enough in their respective roles of the Princesse de Bouillon and the stage manager Michonnet. After that season, Bing quietly had the sets and costumes placed in storage, and nothing was said at the time about future revivals of the opera.

For Tebaldi the situation was far more serious than a few "off-nights" and some less than warm notices in the press. She was keenly aware that something had gone wrong in her singing, and resolved not to perform in public again until such time as the problem was resolved to her own satisfaction. She kept, for the next year, the lowest of public "profiles," never being seen at the opera or anywhere else, cancelling engagements, receiving few visitors and giving no interviews. To this day, Tebaldi dislikes discussing that dark year, and one senses the anguish that she underwent. Her entire adult life had been directed toward singing, and singing with what many called one of the most beautiful voices in operatic history. Suddenly, she seemed unable to sing with ease or beauty of tone.

One course seemed obvious to Tebaldi: she needed to discover what had gone wrong. She contacted a voice teacher to whom she had been introduced in Italy several years before, Ugo de Caro. According to Tebaldi, she began restudying her art, as diligently as in the conservatory years before. It appeared that a basically insignificant flaw in her breathing technique had eventually caused strain to set in. After months of hard work, this problem was corrected and the voice returned.

Meanwhile, during her months of absence from the public eye, people on both sides of the operatic footlights expressed concern about her health, wondering when, or if, she would return to the stage and what the results would be if she did. The Met's 1963-64 season opened, with a new production of *Aïda* that starred Birgit Nilsson and Carlo Bergonzi under Georg Solti's baton. To the relief of many, Tebaldi's name appeared in its accustomed place on the roster. Yet the management would not say when she would sing or in what roles, nor would it definitely guarantee that she'd sing at all that year. A "good luck" telegram from the soprano arrived at the Met in time to be displayed on the bulletin board in the executive office of the opera house on opening night, but that cable was Tebaldi's only public gesture during the fall.

By late winter, a hopeful sign appeared. Renata Tebaldi's

name continued to be listed on a Philadelphia Lyric Opera advertisement for *La Bohème* on March 11, 1964. Then New York fans' hopes were aroused by a Met announcement that Tebaldi would sing her first Mimi of the season at the broadcast matinee of March 14, four days after the Philadelphia performance of the same opera. Of course, it is not uncommon in the world of opera to use the name of a popular artist to sell tickets to a performance even if that artist's participation is in doubt. The Met has often employed this tactic, hoping that the star will appear but knowing that it does not have to refund money if he or she does happen to cancel. However, as the dates for the two performances approached, Tebaldi's name remained on the posters. It appeared as if she would try things out in Philadelphia and then go on to her Met appearance, a challenge made infinitely harder since the latter performance would be broadcast and heard by millions throughout the nation.

The Philadelphia *Bohème* went very well indeed. A number of friends and admirers made the ninety-mile trip from New York, and they, along with the Philadelphia opera lovers, gave Tebaldi a long and cordial welcome when she stepped out onstage. Their greeting helped steady Tebaldi's nerves and she sang a strong and charming performance, animating Mimi with her winsome smile and singing with a voice lighter and far fresher in sound than she had displayed a year previously at the Metropolitan.

Cheered by her reception and by the quality of the Philadelphia performance, Tebaldi returned to her Manhattan apartment to wait out the three days remaining until her reappearance at the Met. Tebaldi, who denies that she was particularly nervous on the occasion of her Met debut, recalls being awed by the prospect of her return to the venerable stage of the old opera house. "For me," she says, "it was like a second debut!" Anyone who has ever taken part in a performance of any sort, even on the most amateur level, knows the tortures one can put oneself through waiting to appear on the stage or concert platform. It does not matter how well one has prepared for the performance, or whether or not rehearsals have gone well. Waiting backstage, the artist is acutely conscious of all he or she is expected to attain during the performance, and equally (and painfully) aware of the many things that may go wrong. Although outsiders may think that a performer who has attained prominence and a mastery of his art does not experience such nervousness or stage fright, this is not all the case. The greater one has been, the greater one is expected to be each time a performance is given. A well-known Metropolitan tenor who has sung leading roles at the Met and elsewhere but who cannot be said to be in the "superstar" category once expressed sympathy for Franco Corelli, a "superstar" who is notoriously tense before and during performances. "When I go out there to sing," the American tenor told me, "I know that my reputation is that of a pretty good singer. If I have a good night, fine, everyone bravos and goes home happy. And, if I have not so good an evening, people may be disappointed, but no one thinks it's the end of the world. But when Corelli walks out to sing, he knows that on every piece of publicity ever written about him, he is proclaimed as the 'world's greatest tenor' and thus the pressure on him to succeed is many times greater than the pressure I feel. I always give my best out there, but at least I don't have the added hassle of having to be the world's greatest tenor each time I open my mouth."

And so it was with Renata Tebaldi. Not that she ever billed herself as the world's greatest soprano. To many, of course, she was the best in the world, and no one, least of all Tebaldi, would dispute that up until the previous year her career had been basically a succession of triumphs. Every audience for which she sang acclaimed her, and every opera house or concert hall where she had sung welcomed her back as often as she chose to appear. Her records sold voluminously, and in the United States, concert managers referred to her as "Miss Sold-Out," since tickets were always gone long before her performances.

All of this must have weighed heavily on Tebaldi's mind as she traveled to the Metropolitan early that Saturday afternoon in March. Thoughts of past performances at the Met, and, one imagines, memories of the previous season's painful *Adriana Lecouvreurs* were also present. Tebaldi habitually arrives at the opera house about 75 minutes before a performance and prays quietly in her dressing room before getting into costume and vocalizing. One can assume that the prayers were especially fervent that afternoon, and that when she was done praying and had turned to the little technical chores that opera singers must see to before each performance, she was especially excited by the prospects of this extraordinary afternoon. Great artists may entertain certain fears about the unknown quantity—and quality—of the performance they are about to give, but they also realize that when they perform not everything is left to chance—obviously, preparation, technique, and experience count for a great deal, and Tebaldi was able to summon all the resources of her art when her turn came to sing.

Meanwhile, the sold-out house buzzed with activity. Even if many of the subscribers were unaware of the special poignancy of the *Bohème* they were about to hear, there were hundreds present who understood exactly what the afternoon meant for Tebaldi, and it can be said that the performance meant much to them as well. Then too, there was the vast radio audience, invisible to the cast but very much in their minds.

Milton Cross, hosting the broadcast, made no special reference to the fact that Tebaldi was making her first Metropolitan appearance in thirteen months, nor did he mention that her Rodolfo, Hungarian tenor Sandor Konya, was singing that role for the first time in his Metropolitan career. At last the performance began, and, it seems most likely that few in the audience, whether in the opera house or at home, paid a great deal of attention to the fifteen minutes of exposition that precede the departure of Marcello, Schaunard, and Colline for the Café Momus, leaving Rodolfo alone in the Parisian garret. Mimi's knock at the door was heard at last, and, playing back the tape today, the listener can sense the audience's tension as they wait to hear Tebaldi's first note. Mimi's first two lines are sung offstage, and she does not actually appear until the tenor has opened the door on his line "Ecco." As Tebaldi entered onto the stage a roar went up in the audience quite unlike any that had erupted in the house in recent memory. Polite applause became enthusiastic clapping as soon as the full audience could see Tebaldi. The more vociferous fans began yelling "Brava Renata" and the cheering went on undiminished for several moments—and all of this before Tebaldi had sung a single phrase at full voice. (Mimi grows weak and faints seconds after her entrance; thus she has to sing her opening lines *piano* and doesn't begin singing at full volume until she realizes that she has dropped the key to her room, on the words "O sventata, sventata! La chiave della stanza . . .") Maestro Cleva had signaled to his musicians to stop playing while the ovation was at its peak; there was simply no point in going on. Knowing well how to gauge such demonstrations of affection, Cleva began the performance again as soon as the cheering began to die down, but several more lines were muffled by the most vociferous Tebaldiani. When the audience had at last regained its collective composure, Mimi had fainted! Soon enough, though, Konya "revived" her with a little wine, and the cognoscenti knew that Tebaldi was about to meet her first real test of the day. On the line "O sventata, sventata . . ." her voice rang out with its wonted clarity and freedom. Tebaldi had returned in seemingly fine voice. Moments later, of course, comes Mimi's aria "Mi chiamono Mimi," and this would provide the audience with its first opportunity that day to judge Tebaldi's sustained vocalism. By the time the generous applause for this well-loved piece had died down, it could be seen (or heard!) that Tebaldi's voice had altered somewhat from its pre-1963 sound. Still satiny and undiminished in beauty throughout the middle range, the higher notes had taken on a certain metallic quality, suggesting that some of the youthful bloom had faded. Still, there remained the generous amplitude of sound, the opulent breath control, and, above all, a sense of undiminished—in fact, increased—artistry. Mimi is Puccini's most real and most charming heroine. Like her more heroic "sisters," Tosca, Cio-cio-san, Manon, et al., Mimi does not survive, but her personal tragedy is as gentle and low-keyed as she is modest and frail. Tebaldi's performance that day brought out all of Mimi's endearing qualities, and the later acts were fraught with the drama of Mimi and Rodolfo's unhappy love and her increasingly ill health.

Upon the conclusion of the opera Tebaldi received an ovation at least twenty minutes long. The afternoon had been a grand success and brought a disturbing chapter of the Tebaldi career to a happy ending—or, more properly, to a new beginning, as the soprano now felt ready to continue her Met appearances as well as to sing elsewhere and make recordings.

Tebaldi's return to the stage was not neglected by the newspapers and other media. Writing in the *New York Times,* Raymond Ericson seemed pleased to have Tebaldi back, and understanding of the changes that were taking place in her singing: "By the end of her aria 'Mi chiamono Mimi,' the audience was able to relax in the knowledge that the soprano was in fine form. If there were reservations about the quality of her voice, they could not detract much from the over-all impressiveness of her performance. Miss Tebaldi's voice will probably never recapture the plush warmth and richness that once made it the most beautiful of its kind among modern singers. In the upper register at loud volumes, the voice now becomes somewhat hard and edgy—although this can be remarkably effective at peak dramatic moments. Otherwise, her voice was lovely, and, as the opera progressed and it warmed up, it developed that wonted, melting quality. The singer was always in control of her singing, and she molded the phrases with care. When she had a legitimate reason to do so, she spun out the musical line lovingly and ravishingly. Add to Miss Tebaldi's vocal blandishments the undefinable authority she carries as a true prima donna and her charm of personality, and the extended ovations she received at the end of each act can be understood. The soprano seemed happy at her reception, smiling, waving, and gesturing repeatedly to the audience."

In the next day's *New York Herald Tribune,* Alan Rich headlined his article "Renata Tebaldi Returns—A Great Singer Despite Flaws" and went on to discuss the previous day's performance: "much of what she did on Saturday afternoon was in the great Tebaldi tradition. There were phrases throughout the performance that were exquisite beyond any question. Also beyond any question was the fact that she had overcome whatever had thrown her so badly off a year ago. Her Mimi was recognizably a Tebaldi performance, and, at least in its broad outlines, an extremely moving and great performance. But . . . for all its new security, and for all its enchanting lightness and flexibility, the voice also had many faults that are extremely disturbing. Throughout the afternoon Miss Tebaldi produced sounds at the upper end of her range at volume that were extremely shrill and metallic. They were not passing faults, either; the quality seemed to be deeply imbedded in the voice itself, and changed little as the performance wore on. These are sad words to write, because Renata Tebaldi remains one of the supremely gifted singers in the canon of Italian opera. The majesty of her musical and dramatic conception, the innate feeling for lyric flow that has ennobled her art from her first appearances on the operatic state . . . these are things to cherish and they were completely in evidence at this performance. If Miss Tebaldi were to make her debut now, in her present vocal condition, they would still be recognized as elements of a sovereign performer. But, because these elements are so great, the negative side of her singing is all the more tragic to contemplate."

Thus, amidst the general and sincere rejoicing that Tebaldi was back, and still a very great artist, there was a less happy sense that time had begun to take its toll on Tebaldi's voice. Still, compared to virtually any standard but that of her own former level of singing, she was in superb form. Her confidence in her own work had to a very great extent returned, and her relationship with live audiences, always one of rare feeling and mutual sympathy, took an an especially personal character which has remained there to the present day. During the next few weeks, as she added *Tosca* and *Otello* to her working repertoire, she seemed more touched than ever by the thunderous receptions given her. In fact, she often burst into tears at the conclusion of an act, or even after an aria such as *Tosca*'s "Vissi d'arte" when the audience poured out their affection in sustained volleys of cheers. It is easy to wax maudlin over these scenes, but the relationship between Renata Tebaldi and her audiences has always been one of the few such phenomena that can genuinely be characterized by the word "love". There are many other highly popular singers who regularly thrill audiences, and yet the cheering, however strong, does not match the very real warmth which flows between the spectators and Tebaldi. Perhaps one senses that Renata Tebaldi, more than other artists, is especially buoyed up by these ovations, that they are highly valued by her as something beyond simple feedback that she has done her job well. Therefore, knowing that the feeling of appreciation is returned, one tends to applaud and even scream "Brava" to a far greater extent than may be merited by a given performance.

For whatever reason—not the least of which were the even stronger performances that Tebaldi gave as the 63-64 season wound up—the cheering continued. It was especially great on March 23. As the auditorium readied itself for Tebaldi's first New York *Tosca* in at least four years, with Gobbi returning to sing Scarpia, Rudolf Bing appeared before the footlights. "Miss Tebaldi is quite well," Bing told the startled audience. "But Mr. Barry Morell is unable to sing the role of Mario tonight, and we wish to thank Mr. Franco Corelli for agreeing to sing on very short notice." Bing's last words were partially obscured by the roar that went up at the mention of Corelli's name. It is rare indeed for a tenor of Corelli's calibre to substitute for a lesser known and far less brilliant colleague. Thus, with the electrifying presence of Gobbi to add further excitement to the occasion, Tebaldi and Corelli took up once again a partnership that had begun a year earlier in unhappy circumstances, but now blossomed into one of the most exciting combinations ever to fire the stage of the Met.

If anything, Tebaldi seemed surer of herself at the first *Tosca* than at the *Bohème*. She phrased as expansively as ever, but there was an ever increasing dramatic fire to her singing. That night, Tebaldi elected to sing the words "E avanti a lui tremava tutta Roma" rather than speaking them, a practice employed by many other sopranos, including Tebaldi in more recent years. Sung with icy disdain, following the lava-like projection of much of the earlier music, the effect was stunning.

Tebaldi sang two more performances of *Tosca* that season. At the next performance, four nights later, Barry Morrell returned to his scheduled place in the cast, and Tebaldi alternated between extreme tenderness for her Mario and the venom she reserved for Scarpia, sung by Gobbi once again. At that performance, I was standing at the extreme front of the right side of the auditorium (at the old house orchestra standees stood all around the horseshoe, and the front of the side areas, while not offering a full view of the stage, allowed a close-up view of roughly half the playing area). The high degree of concentration on the part of both Tebaldi and Gobbi was awesome. Tebaldi seemed to jump involuntarily "out of her skin" when Gobbi touched her bosom insinuatingly as he made her his final offer to spare Mario's life.

That Tebaldi was deeply aware of her audience, in spite of her immersion in her role, was demonstrated by her bursting into tears of joy when she received an enormous burst of applause on her entrance, and also after the "Vissi d'arte." During the latter ovation, poor Gobbi was forced to remain staring out the window of the set into the nothingness of the backstage wall, for he was too considerate to interrupt the applause by moving downstage until the cheering had faded away.

Tebaldi sang several performances of Desdemona that spring, including two during the Met's World's Fair season in May. This was the precursor of the June Festivals the Met was to stage at Lincoln Center in years to come. As 1964 was the four hundredth anniversary of Shakespeare's birth, the Met celebrated during both its regular and special seasons by staging Verdi's three Shakespearean operas. Thus Tebaldi at last had an opportunity to appear in the Eugene Berman production of *Otello* that had been designed for her the year before. The World's Fair season was plagued by an early heat wave, and Tebaldi was forced to sing in Berman's heavy costumes under hot stage lights in "90-degrees-in-the-shade" conditions. Still, the performances were successful, with Tebaldi singing as affecting a "Willow Song" as ever, and looking slenderer and more youthful than in previous performances of the role. Once the Met season was ended, Renata returned to Italy for vacation, and then went to London to record an aria recital for Decca-London, which represented her first time before the microphones in about two years.

Tebaldi commenced her 1964-65 Metropolitan season with an appearance in a gala concert for the Metropolitan's Production Fund on a Sunday night in November. Renata sang Mimi in the first act of *La Bohème,* Joan Sutherland appeared in the first act of *La Traviata,* and the evening opened with the first act of Strauss's *Der Rosenkavalier,* sung by Elizabeth Schwarzkopf as the Marschallin and Lisa Della Casa as Octavian. This *Rosenkavalier* excerpt provided the occasion for the one and only stage appearance of Tebaldi's little poodle, Mr. New. During the Marschallin's *leveé,* an animal vendor offers the princess a small dog. At the last moment, the agency responsible for bringing the dog used in the production to the opera house slipped up. The stage manager found himself without the diminutive canine who had a well-known and amusing "bit" in the first act of the Strauss comedy. What was to be done? Someone backstage knew that the Tebaldi entourage had already arrived, with New in tow. An emissary sought out Tebaldi and asked her if she would "lend" New to the company for the occasion. Tebaldi was delighted to comply, and so her frisky little grey dog was allowed to prance around the stage while Tebaldi, as proud as Madame Rose in *Gypsy,* enjoyed the spectacle from the wings. From all accounts, New went through his paces as if he were born to them, and, Strauss' tinkling musical joke to the contrary, did not disgrace himself when the animal vendor assured his potential customer that the dog was perfectly trained. The stage manager saw to it that New received the $10 fee that would have gone to the owner of the originally scheduled pet, but his manager, Mme. Tebaldi, contributed the salary to the Met's Employees Benevolent Fund. His debut accomplished. Mr. New retired to Tebaldi's dressing room as the soprano prepared for her seasonal return.

With her New York appearances launched on a festive note, Tebaldi settled into her Manhattan apartment, prepared to sing in such operas as *Tosca, Simon Boccanegra,* and *Otello*. In general, her appearances went well. Her fans noticed that she was still visibly moved at each demonstration of appreciation from the audience. Even though her return to singing could now be considered fully successful, Renata seemed poignantly cognizant of the reasons for her recent year-long absence, and each performance seemed like a challenge to lay to rest the ghosts of the not-so-distant past. Entrance applause brought forth tears, as did warm applause following such an aria as "Vissi d'arte". In contrast to years past, Tebaldi was expected by the management to carry virtually alone all the burdens of great singing at each performance. Warren had died, Bastianini was seriously ill for much of the season, and Del Monaco had left the country; owing to poor planning, many of the casts with whom she sang were not up to previous standards. *Otello* was sung that season not by the likes of Del Monaco or McCracken (the American tenor sang but one performance of the role that year) but by such comparative nonentities as Arturo Sergi and Dimitir Uzunof, while her colleagues in *Tosca* too often included Morell and Merrill—the latter an indisputedly gifted baritone but not a Scarpia of the Gobbi or Warren class. There were, however, one or two *Bohèmes* with Corelli, and *Boccanegra* was as a rule far more solidly cast. Tebaldi sang a stunning duet with Anselmo Colzani, who made the Doge a touching and human figure, and Giorgio Tozzi contributed an imposing Fiesco.

The 1964-65 season was, incidentally, the year of Callas's return to the Met, but those who either feared or longed for a head-on clash between the two artists were disappointed, since by the time Callas returned, in mid-March, Tebaldi had already completed her engagement.

Tebaldi sang quite well that season. Virtually all traces of the occasional hesitancy that had marked her first appearances the previous March were gone. Her Tosca's grew ever more authoritatively dramatic, and her Amelia Grimaldi in *Boccanegra* developed a new regal quality. Vocally, Tebaldi retained much of the flexibility of her voice, although the tendency continued for notes above High A to sound metallic. The broadcast performance of *Boccanegra* on January 30 came within one day of the tenth anniversary of her Met debut, and but two days before her birthday. Therefore, when she appeared for her solo bow at the end of the day, several dozen Tebaldiani rushed to the front of the orchestra and sang "Happy Birthday" to her. She seemed entirely surprised. The line outside the Met's stage door after that performance was big enough to surge into the street and snarl traffic for more than an hour.

Tebaldi made one postseason appearance with the Met. The company had taken over managing the summer concerts given at City College's Lewisohn Stadium in upper Manhattan. Renata was asked to sing at the opening concert in June. She had sung there before, in a 1957 summer concert that had gone very well, and therefore was pleased enough to help inaugurate the Met's latest venture. Looking more beautiful than ever, with her long red hair offsetting a very becoming green gown (Harold C. Schonberg compared her to Botticelli's Venus in his review the next day in the *Times*) Tebaldi treated the capacity crowd of well over 10,000 people to a program that included "Ritorna vincitor," "Tacea la notte placida," "Un bel di," "Voi lo sapete," and Rossini's song cycle "La regata veneziana." Following the concert, she left for England, where she recorded *Don Carlo*.

The 1965-66 season was the last at the old Metropolitan Opera House. Renata was not given a new production, but was invited to sing three of her best roles, Mimi, Tosca, and Maddalena in *Andrea Chenier*. Her New York season began the week before Christmas with a sizzling performance of *Tosca*, in which she matched wits with the Scarpia of Gabriel Bacquier, while the ubiquitous Konya appeared as Mario. The first performance went well, with Tebaldi looking radiant in a series of new costumes, including a particularly glamorous rose-colored gown for the second act. Bacquier proved to be the finest Scarpia at the Met since Gobbi, and the second act flashed with electrifying excitement. Renata accidentally dropped the knife she would use to murder Scarpia at the first performance, but, glancing quickly at her enemy to see if he had noticed (Bacquier obligingly had not!) she picked up the recalcitrant weapon and turned the moment into a triumph of improvisation. Her voice that night combined a great deal of her old warmth of sound with new dramatic power.

The following week Tebaldi sang a Mimi, in the company of Konya's Rodolfo, and Heidi Krall's Musetta, that brought back memories of her first seasons in New York, as her voice gave off its richest glow. Not that the performance went all that smoothly. Cleva, the conductor, had suffered heart seizures that were growing steadily more severe. On several occasions during the first half of that season, he had had to cancel; finally he had to withdraw for a protracted rest. That night, December 30, the venerable Italian maestro suffered a seizure during the first act of *Bohème,* but somehow managed to finish the act, when he was replaced by an assistant conductor.

For many, Tebaldi's most eagerly awaited role that season was Maddalena, which she hadn't sung in New York for six years. The first performance was a Metropolitan Opera Guild benefit on Sunday, January 30. Her partners that evening were Franco Corelli and Anselmo Colzani, who replaced the originally announced Tito Gobbi, while Lamberto Gardelli made his local debut conducting. January 30 was the snowiest, iciest day thus far that winter. A dismal, heavy wind swept people across treacherously slippery pavements. In spite of the elements, a full complement of standees formed their line in front of the opera house by dawn and we (yes, I was among the earliest risers that day) waited patiently until six o'clock in the evening for tickets to be sold. Like the *Boccanegra* performance the previous season, this *Chenier* marked a Tebaldi birthday and Metropolitan debut anniversary, and many of her fans were prepared to mark the occasion with particularly vociferous cheers. Then too, Corelli has a very strong, loyal coterie of fans, and the atmosphere inside the auditorium that night could hardly have been more festive.

Looking back on that performance, nothing dissuades me from my original opinion that it was the single most exciting performance that I witnessed at the old Met. Both Tebaldi and Corelli were in splendid voice that evening, holding high notes longer than one would have thought even that pair capable of in the duets, and Tebaldi sang a "La mamma morta" that ranked with the best of her work down through the years. The supporting cast was especially fine, and Gardelli, who unfortunately did not remain at the Met very long, led a dynamically animated performance that was repeated the following Saturday on a broadcast matinee. Meanwhile, the fans inside the opera house couldn't seem to get Tebaldi and Corelli to take enough curtain calls. The cheering went on for nearly half an hour after the opera ended, with the Tebaldiani again singing "Happy Birthday, dear Renata."

April 16 marked the last night that the old Met would resound to operatic music (the Bolshoi Ballet was the final tenant before the theatre was torn down), and Bing decided to close the era with a grand gala concert that would feature most if not all the company's leading artists and also honor surviving artists of the recent past. As Tebaldi and Corelli were a favorite combination at the box office, it was decided that the two would be paired at the gala farewell. They chose to sing the great love duet from act two of *Manon Lescaut*, although Corelli had never sung that opera at the Met. Framed against the grand ballroom setting from the Met's *Eugen Onegin* production, Tebaldi and Corelli made a handsome couple, pouring all their forces of lyric passion into Puccini's music. Even coming in a segment of the concert that featured Leontyne Price singing "D'amor sull'ali rosee" and Nilsson singing the "Immolation Scene" from *Gotterdammerung*, their duet was considered by all a major event of the evening. Tebaldi returned to the stage with the entire company one last time to sing "Auld Lang Syne" at the evening's end. During an intermission that night, she was introduced to two of

Broadway's leading ladies, Ethel Merman and Barbra Streisand.

In addition to Tebaldi's Metropolitan performances, Tebaldi took part in a Carnegie Hall presentation of the American Opera Society, Boito's *Mefistofele*. This performance predated the New York City Opera's visually splendid revival by three years. It was the first performance of Boito's opera since before World War II, and the fact that its cast included three prominent Metropolitan artists, Tebaldi, Bergonzi, and Nicolai Ghiaurov (the bass, like the performance's conductor, Lamberto Gardelli, had recently debuted at the Met) pointed up the absurdity of its exclusion from the Metropolitan's repertoire. Tebaldi, as noted in the more detailed discussion of the performance in the Recordings section, portrayed both Margherita and Helen of Troy.

The Met continued its operation of Lewisohn Stadium in the summer of 1966 (in years following, it suspended concerts there in favor of free concerts in various city parks). Tebaldi sang there twice: once in a concert performance of *La Bohème*—in which she and her colleagues were forced to compete with firecrackers set off by early celebrants of the July 4 holiday—and a solo concert with the Met's orchestra on the closing night of the summer season. It was at this sold-out affair that Tebaldi, after singing a potpourri of standard arias, surprised and charmed the audience by singing, as an encore, the Rodgers and Hammerstein song "If I Loved You" from *Carousel*. It was the first time she had sung publicly in English, and the crowd sent up a roar of approval as soon as the music was recognized. Her accent was noticeable, but adorable, and the cheering was so great that she sang the song through again. Since that time, "If I Loved You" has become a signature tune for Tebaldi's concerts in the United States and London, and she has recorded it as well. It proved to be a lovely way of ending a concert and a season, and incidentally marked her last appearance in New York before singing at the new Met.

The Metropolitan Opera's move to the new opera house at Lincoln Center represented the fruition of dreams of general managers, board members, and other patrons of the company stretching back at least sixty years, when Giulio Gatti-Casazza, who became general manager in 1905, was assured that there would be a new opera house within a very few years. The old theatre, for all its fabled aura of history and great operatic performances, was inadequate for modern presentation of operas: its backstage facilities were cramped to the point of near nonexistence, its sightlines were poor (even if the acoustics were fabulous), and it represented a veritable mass of fire risks and assorted safety hazards. Thus the move to Lincoln Center represented a virtual leap into the future insofar as the creation and production of opera was concerned.

The staging facilities of the new house are among the most advanced of our day, and Rudolf Bing wanted to make full use of them in his first season at Lincoln Center, as if to christen the new theatre in a blaze of operatic brilliance. Hence, Bing commissioned nine new productions, including two American operas that would receive their world premieres that season. Then, in Santa Claus fashion, he began to distribute these plums among his artists. As the opening night was to be a tribute to American opera, the cast for the world premiere of Samuel Barber's *Antony and Cleopatra* was made up of native talent. Leontyne Price had well earned the honor of inaugurating the new house, and her costars included Justino Diaz, Jess Thomas, and Rosalind Elias, while Thomas Schippers conducted. Anna Moffo, Robert Merrill, and Bruno Prevedi appeared in a new staging of *La Traviata*, which replaced the Guthrie-Smith-Gerard version built around Tebaldi's Violetta nine years earlier. Birgit Nilsson, Leonie Rysanek, and Regina Resnik starred in Strauss's *Elektra*, while another Strauss opera, *Die Frau ohne Schatten*, received a spectacular production. Sung by a brilliant cast—Rysanek, Ludwig, Dalis, King, Berry—and conducted by Karl Böhm, it ranks as one of the finest achievements in the company's ninety-year history. Other productions included *Peter Grimes* (conducted by Colin Davis, staged by Guthrie, with Jon Vickers in the title role), *Lohengrin*, and the world premiere of Marvin David Levy's *Mourning Becomes Electra*. What was offered to

Tebaldi, a year or more before the move uptown, was a new production of Amilcare Ponchielli's *La Gioconda.* This mad, splendidly melodious opera has been an audience favorite and a singer's delight ever since its first performance. Critics dismiss it for its absurd plot (one of Hugo's lesser melodramas was distorted through the wit of Arrigo Boito, who under a pseudonym fashioned from it a libretto that reads almost like a parody of grand opera). The Met's most recent production dated from the Gatti-Casazza era, although Bing had had it repainted during the early years of his administration when Zinka Milanov sang the title role, arguably the heaviest and most taxing in the Italian repertoire. Milanov had sung *Gioconda* from the early 1940s right up through 1963, when she had alternated in the opera with Eileen Farrell. Now Milanov had retired and the enormously gifted Farrell had also left the company. Renata Tebaldi, as the house's leading Italian soprano, and one whose voice had begun to take on the qualities of a dramatic soprano as well, seemed the only choice for the role in the new production. "Seemed" is a key word; Tebaldi, Italian as can be and admittedly charismatic, was originally a lyric or *lirico spinto* soprano, and had always seemed content to veer away from the heavier roles. Wagner, except for his most lyric roles, Eva, Elsa, and Elisabeth, never tempted her, and critics as far back as 1955 had noticed that even in the role of Maddalena she seemed to be driving her voice to its fullest physical limits. Tebaldi had never sung a full performance of *Gioconda* onstage (only the duet "L'amo come il fulgor del creato" at a Chicago Lyric Opera concert in 1956); while she had recorded "Suicidio" on her 1964 recital disk, she had several years earlier declined to sing the role on London-Decca's recording (the task fell eventually to Anita Cerquetti).

Tebaldi herself recollects that she was at first dubious about *Gioconda* and accepted the proposal only after a great deal of thought and discussion of the matter with her vocal advisor, De Caro. She then set about learning the role completely, working the part into her voice so that she would appear comfortable singing it, learning how to pace herself (Gioconda's heaviest work comes in the final thirty minutes of the long and complex opera) so that she could shine in the "Suicidio" and thereafter.

Gioconda unquestionably represented a turning point in Tebaldi's singing. In itself a remarkable achievement, a blending of intensely dramatic singing with beautifully expressive phrasing, Tebaldi's *Gioconda* revealed her as a vocal actress of unstinting passion and force, qualities that contrasted with the soft and almost delicate feminine charm that she projected in other roles. Still, *Gioconda* took a very definite toll on her voice. Her singing was never again as exquisitely lyrical in such roles as Mimi, Manon Lescaut, and Desdemona as it was before she sang the Ponchielli heroine. Many individual *Gioconda* performances were superb, with a fine balance kept between dramatic exaggeration and subtle expression in Tebaldi's singing. On other occasions, she tended to overuse chest tones while a dangerous stridency affected her high notes, still, the general effect of the *Gioconda*s was one of stunning power and vivid excitement. Wearing a seductive-looking, long, black wig, and multicolored gypsy costume designed by Beni Montresor, Renata was the loveliest Gioconda in memory, and at her best was one of the most prodigiously sung ones as well.

What lingers in the mind, though, is the question of how her career might have gone if, instead of accepting the new production offered her, she had refused and asked instead for a new *Bohème* or *Tosca*, both of which merited new stagings.

The new Gioconda, designed by Montresor, staged by Margherita Wallman, and conducted by Cleva (recovered, for the time being, from his heart ailment), merged the vocal talents of Tebaldi with those of Corelli as Enzo, MacNeil as Barnaba, Biserka Cvejic as Laura, Belen Amparán as la Cieca and Cesare Siepi as Alvise. The opera was the second given at the new Metropolitan, with its premiere postponed three days as an aftereffect of a short strike by orchestra members. Coincidentally, in 1883, *La Gioconda* was the first "novelty" presented at the newborn Metropolitan Opera House. Now, eighty-three years later, it became the first work from the standard repertoire to grace the new auditorium at

Lincoln Center. Due to the unprecedented demand for tickets, people camped out in sleeping bags for days in order to buy seats or standing room for the first performances.

Critics in general praised the colorful designs that Montresor provided for the opera, and in general they liked the singing. Tebaldi's performance impressed all as far as her concern for dramatic expression, but the sound of her voice aroused some controversy. Harold C. Schonberg, writing in the *Times*, was not among the most impressed that evening.

"Always a slow starter, she gained in confidence as she went along, and by the third act she was producing tones—rather hard in quality—of ear-splitting intensity."

Irving Kolodin delved somewhat more deeply into the performance in his column in the *Saturday Review* of October 8: "neither the richness nor abundance of the sound that [Tebaldi] once possessed is any longer at her command, but she has become a much more thoughtful artist, who puts her good looks and still luminous 'star' quality to the service of the role she plays rather than assuming a dominance of the scene as she once did. [In the "Suicidio"] she applied all the ounces of artistry at her command to equal the pounds of persuasion she used to assert by voice alone."

Interestingly, Winthrop Sargent, reviewing the first performance of *La Gioconda* for *The New Yorker*, felt that her singing was as fine as ever. "[Tebaldi's] singing did not in any way show the defects that I have noticed for the past several years. She had recovered her voice completely and sang as well as I have ever heard her sing, which is saying a great deal . . . . she was as passionate and uninhibited a Gioconda as anyone could wish."

Gioconda was a great hit with the public, and opera fans who were not subscribers to the Met queued up at the house for last-minute ticket returns, often paying cruelly inflated prices to "scalpers" in order to get in. Such was the allure of the new opera house that thousands of people who knew or cared little about the lyric art fought like tigers to attend a performance, making nearly everything a sell-out. For the *Giocondas*, however, it may safely be said that most of the people who thronged the Met's lobby in the hopes of getting in were attracted by the presence of Tebaldi and Corelli in the cast.

There were any number of great moments in Tebaldi's performance. Considered as a whole, her Giocondas exuded enough allure and dramatic power to dominate the action whenever she appeared. Her singing had the volume necessary to penetrate Ponchielli's brash orchestration, yet her command of the *pianissimo* was very much in evidence, as on so well-known a phrase as "Enzo adorato, ah come t'amo" in the first act, and especially in her "Son la Gioconda" in act two. The sight of Tebaldi regally brooding by the sea garbed in a gorgeous golden cloak, which greeted the audience as the curtain rose on Act Four, invariably drew applause. What followed, more often than not, was thirty-five minutes of fascinatingly dramatic and forceful singing, in a scene in which all of Gioconda's many conflicting feelings come into play: tenderness, bitterness, devotion, jealousy, and so on. By force of personality as much as by the handsomeness of her singing, Tebaldi dominated even the elements of the performance offered by Corelli, Cvejic (or her alternate, Rosalind Elias), and MacNeil.

One of the finest aspects of her Gioconda was Tebaldi's ability to portray the various self-contradictory sides of her heroine so that the character seemed credible. Particularly moving, in the first act, was this Gioconda's tender and solicitous treatment of her "mother," La Cieca. Given Tebaldi's own deep feelings for her mother, it was probably inevitable that these scenes were so touchingly handled, but for whatever reasons, their effect was great.

That first season, 1966-67, Tebaldi performed Gioconda more than a dozen times at the Metropolitan and eight more times on tour. The stage crews were still learning how to operate the complex new backstage machinery, and, due to an accident at a dress rehearsal of *Antony and Cleopatra,* the stage's revolving turntable was out of operation. This caused many delays—one night the first intermission was ninety minutes long, and Rudolf Bing himself helped set each new scene; Tebaldi sang "Suicidio" that night at 1 AM. One performance, in fact, had to be postponed for several days due to mechanical failures on the part of the stage machinery. From time to time there were other difficulties during the *Gioconda* evenings. At one of the later performances Corelli and Tebaldi had a misunderstanding, reflected by angry looks exchanged between the two for the rest of the performance; it also seems to have precipitated Corelli's cancellation of his next *Gioconda,* the broadcast matinee! Corelli consented to sing the opera with Tebaldi on tour, but withdrew from his contract to record the opera with her in the summer. This embryonic feud was settled by the following fall, when Corelli returned to the *Gioconda* cast.

In addition to singing several performances of *La Bohème* in rather awesome contrast to her *Gioconda* duties, Tebaldi sang an additional two performances of the Ponchielli opera at the Met's first June Festival, this time with Richard Tucker as Enzo. At one of these performances, she was visited backstage by the daughter of the Soviet leader Kosygin, who had accompanied her father on his state visit to the United States.

After her summer in Europe, Tebaldi returned to the Metropolitan for the 1967-68 season, in time to sing in the first *Gioconda,* three nights after the season's opening. This time the tenor was Flaviano Labó, who was returning to the Met after an absence of several years. While *Gioconda* continued to delight the public, Renata's voice seemed bigger and more dramatic than ever, though listeners also detected a loss in flexibility and a heavier timbre. These changes did not matter greatly in an opera like *La Gioconda,* but Tebaldi's other principle role that season was *Manon Lescaut,* which she was singing in New York for the first time since 1959, and people wondered what the results would be.

The premiere performance, on October 21, did not begin well. Tebaldi seemed tired upon her entrance, and her singing lacked velvet or ease. Moreover Richard Tucker, singing Des Grieux, was also not at his best. To make matters worse the conductor, Francesco Molinari-Pradelli, managed to get lost during the first duet for soprano and tenor, and had to stop the performance for several moments until he got matters in order. Fortunately, Tebaldi hit her accustomed form by the second act, singing an emotional "In quelle trine morbide" and continuing in a masterful way for the balance of the evening. People did notice, however, that her dramatic conception of Manon had altered with time, and that she now imbued the girl with some of the adult passions more often associated with Gioconda. Vocally, there seemed to be more frequent resort to chest tones as well.

Halfway through her Metropolitan commitment, Tebaldi flew back to Italy to sing her first operatic performance in her native country in five years. She was invited to return to the Teatro San Carlo in Naples, where she had scored some of her earliest great successes, to sing in a new production of *La Gioconda.* The critics were generous and the public, from all accounts, was delirious. Tebaldi was hailed for many curtain calls, and was the recipient of vast numbers of tribute, both floral and vocal.

She then returned to New York where she continued to sing *Gioconda,* occasionally joined, as for the broadcast, by Carlo Bergonzi, who had recorded the opera with her the previous summer, and the brilliant Italian mezzo-soprano Fiorenza Cossotto, who had joined the Metropolitan that season. The broadcast, which represented Tebaldi's last complete *Gioconda* (she would sing the second act at the 1970 gala that celebrated Richard Tucker's twenty-fifth anniversary with the Met), was a stunning performance. Tebaldi was just a little off top form in the first act, where she had some off-pitch moments, but she was able to blend voices magnificently with Cossotto in their second act scene, and sang as vivid and vocally luscious a fourth act as she had ever performed.

Once *Gioconda* was finished, Tebaldi turned again to *Manon Lescaut.* The post-*Gioconda* performances of the Puccini work were stronger than the ones in the earlier part of the season. Now that she no longer had to concentrate on Gioconda, Tebaldi worked toward lightening the quality of her voice. Still—and this was in no way a bad thing—her heightened awareness of the means of showing passion on the stage remained as part of her Manon, and she portrayed the decadent aspects of the character more thoroughly than every before.

Shortly before the *Manon Lescaut* broadcast, Rudolf Bing announced to the public that the next season's opening night would star Renata Tebaldi and Franco Corelli. The opera? *Adriana Lecouvreur.* Even after it was established that Tebaldi had firmly conquered the vocal infirmity that had marred her 1963 *Adriana* performances, it must have rankled her to contemplate that her only unsuccessful appearances at the Met were in her favorite role. Surely she longed for a chance to prove that she could sing the role as well as she sang Mimi, Tosca, or Desdemona.

From Bing's point of view, he had a handsome production of the opera in storage, and since it had only been performed ten times, the sets and costumes looked brand-new. Then too, Renata Tebaldi was still one of the most important members of his company—as a singer of Puccini and *verismo* she remained unchallenged. It had been ten years since her previous, and only, Met opening night (Tebaldi had turned down Bing's offer of an English-language revival of *Eugen Onegin* in 1957, and that plum fell to Lucine Amara), and she had worked hard and well in her most recent new production—the choice of which had been Bing's. It was only fair to reward her with another revival of the Cilea opera. Therefore, contracts were arranged for an opening night performance that would feature the four principals from the 1963 production. The 1968-69 opening night was September 16—three years to the day from the first opening night at Lincoln Center. It would also make operatic history for another reason: by the time the evening ended, that most celebrated of minor musical wars, the Tebaldi-Callas feud, was also at an end. The Saturday before the opening, columnist Leonard Lyons reported that Maria Callas would attend the *Adriana* performance on the following Monday. Therefore, much of the public—or at least the part of it that took interest in such things—was alerted to the very real possibility of a confrontation between the two divas. Tebaldi, evidently not a Lyons reader, missed the column, and if anyone in her household or among her close friends had read it, nothing was said to her.

Monday, September 16 was a warm and sunny late summer day, and by early evening ticket holders, sightseers, and those who hoped to buy last-minute returned tickets converged upon Lincoln Center. Shortly after the doors opened, at 7:30, a familiar and stunning figure made her entrance, wearing a black gown and adorned with gold and rubies—Maria Callas. Callas, escorted by Metropolitan board members, was swiftly propelled to the general manager's box. Word had leaked backstage and virtually all of the members of the *Adriana* cast knew of Callas's presence, but Tebaldi's dressing room door, closed while she finished her preparations, was an effective barrier. Besides, no one backstage was willing to be the one to let Tebaldi know!

At eight o'clock, the lights dimmed for the customary singing of the "Star-Spangled Banner," then raised once more to allow the photographers from the various news media to take pictures of the assembled audience. The house lights dimmed again, but before Fausto Cleva could begin the performance, someone yelled "Brava, Callas." This harebrained shout brought on an equally frivolous volley of "Viva Tebaldi" and for a moment it looked like the gladiators of the fan clubs would finally have their opportunity to do battle. Fortunately, the commotion spent itself after a few seconds, and the opera began. Tebaldi, still snug in her dressing room, had no idea that her "rival" was at the Met.

The performance began, and the rather vacuous first ten minutes of action prior to Adriana's entrance progressed smoothly—although it is doubtful that the audience was very attentive. Many wondered what would happen upon Tebaldi's first entrance. Would the fans create another disturbance? As it happened, everyone was well behaved. Tebaldi made her entrance sumptuously garbed, looking slimmer and lovelier than ever, and posed gracefully in the doorway of the stage setting until the music, drowned out by the brava-shouting, continued. Before she could sing a note, Tebaldi nearly lost her balance on a short flight of steps, but Anselm Colzani caught her arm quickly and she proceeded, seemingly unperturbed, to begin her aria. From then on, all went well. Tebaldi was in superior form that night; poised, gliding contentedly through the score, she showed real emotion in the third and fourth acts, and managed Adriana's long death scene (she dies, of course, from sniffing poisoned violets) without overdoing things dramatically. The audience was receptive throughout, and, at the curtain calls, there was the astonishing sight of Maria Callas sitting in the front of Bing's parterre box, applauding enthusiastically, while Renata Tebaldi took her bows. Callas even admonished one celebrity watcher, who had positioned himself directly outside the door of her box, that he ought to have been inside applauding Mme. Tebaldi instead of waiting for her autograph! The audience was enthusiastic, but the Tebaldiani that evening seemed to outnumber the Corelli people. This logistical coup was especially noticeable at the final round of curtain calls, when the Tebaldi group positioned themselves directly at the foot of the orchestra, and shouted themselves hoarse for her each time she appeared. Corelli, who had been in indifferent voice at best that evening, grew a little piqued at what he considered to be the coolness of his reception and abruptly refused to take any more curtain calls, even though the fans were still applauding. In deference to the tenor, the footlights were turned off and the fire curtain lowered.

Whether it was at this point that Callas, still watching from her box seat, decided to go backstage to console Corelli, or whether she had already made up her mind to go backstage to see all the artists, will probably never be known. Backstage she went, however, and presumably she asked Bing on her way there to discover tactfully whether or not Renata would see her.

So Bing, who was also guiding Mayor and Mrs. John Lindsay, deposited Callas and the city's First Couple in Corelli's room and then cautiously knocked at Tebaldi's dressing room door. According to Tebaldi, Bing congratulated her, and then mentioned, with studied casualness, that he had one or two people with him who wanted to meet her—including Callas.

For Tebaldi, the request must have been a numbing shock. She had not spoken directly to Callas in at least fifteen years. In between the Rio concert and the Met *Adriana*, many unpleasant comments had been uttered, attributed to one lady or the other, and opinions had polarized. Furthermore, Callas's vocal problems had increased and in 1968 she was more or less retired from public life, while Tebaldi had surmounted one grave vocal crisis and continued to sing successfully. However her emotions may have been affected by the event, Tebaldi said, simply, "yes" to Bing's request. Callas was asked to enter the dressing room and then she and Tebaldi were face to face. Hardly a word was said. Instead, the two divas reached out for each other and embraced. Tebaldi beamed and Callas was close to tears. Then, for the benefit of the surprised photographers present, Renata and Callas posed, embracing, with the equally stunned Bing between them. It was precisely at this moment that the non-VIP fans were allowed to pour in, and those of us who arrived first were able to witness the reconciliation. One Tebaldiano quipped that now he could play his Callas records openly! Callas herself soon left the backstage area, allowing Tebaldi to enjoy her triumph without competition. So ended the Tebaldi-Callas feud, and since then two ladies have had only kind words to say about the other. The making-up was undeniably fun, and added a further touch of excitement to the badly withering ritual of opening nights at the Metropolitan.

Critic Harold C. Schonberg, who had ranted rather unbecomingly in the *Times* the day before the performance against the choice of *Adriana Lecouvreur* to launch the season, ostentatiously stayed far away from the opera house that night. But his "stand-in," Raymond Ericson, after making what the obligatory remarks about the thinness of the opera, was happy to own up to the fact that Tebaldi had had a fine night: "Tackling [*Adriana*] once again last night, she was much more the Tebaldi of old and she provided much beautiful singing. The music lies well for her, much of it is in the range where the voice retains its familiar velvet. There were some edgy high tones to be sure, but also some of brilliant steeliness. Miss Tebaldi looked regal, and if she is an actress of stately charm rather than temperament, she brings presence to the role." Thus *Adriana,* more happily launched in 1968 than five years earlier, was given thirteen times in New York that season and was taken on the spring tour as well. Corelli sang many of the performances. But on a fateful Saturday in October, he cancelled on three hours' notice, leaving the way open for the debut of the young Spanish tenor Placido Domingo. Domingo, then less than thirty years old, had already become a major artist of the New York City Opera and had appeared in other cities in the United States, Mexico, Israel, and elsewhere. In fact, he was scheduled to make his Metropolitan debut in the same opera four nights later, but Corelli's sudden refusal to perform gave Domingo's debut the touch of drama that helped it become a feature story in newspapers the next day. Domingo had sung with Tebaldi as early in his U.S. career as 1966, when they sang a *La Bohème* in Boston directed by Sarah Caldwell. Domingo's Met career has, of course, prospered, and he immediately became one of that company's top tenors.

In addition to *Adriana,* Renata sang several performances of *Bohème* in 1968-69, and soon took over the title role in the Met's new production—and a most sorely needed one at that—of *Tosca.* This had been unveiled in October with Birgit Nilsson, Corelli, and Gabriel Bacquier in the leading roles. Tebaldi took advantage of the new stage direction to reveal to New York a decidedly altered Tosca. Before her Tosca had been notable for its inherent gentleness of demeanor; now she was a more mature heroine, and certainly a more fiery one than in the past. There were many moments of tenderness, both dramatically and vocally, but these were reserved for Mario, whether sung by Corelli, Domingo, or Tucker. For Scarpia, Tebaldi revealed, and reveled in, a scalding brilliance of sound and fury of gesture that made the second act thrilling to behold. High notes were on the flinty side but they were big and powerful. Moreover, Tebaldi had never before looked as well onstage as she did that season, and the picture of Tosca that she presented was truly that of the most beautiful and exciting diva in Rome, or anywhere else. One performance in April, with Domingo and Colzani, was especially fine.

The June Festival of 1969 was a one-week affair, opened by Tebaldi and Corelli in *Tosca* (Colzani was again the Scarpia, and a fine one) and closed by them in *La Bohème,* a performance that has turned out to be their last—or at least, their most recent—together at the Metropolitan. Before the season ended, it was announced that, in addition to singing Mimi and Tosca once again next season, Renata Tebaldi would add Minnie in *La Fanciulla del West* to the list of her Puccini roles performed in New York. Tebaldi had recorded the opera and also sung it in a radio concert performance in Italy nearly a decade earlier, but this would be her first Minnie in any opera house.

The 1969-70 Metropolitan season became known as the "short season" as it was delayed for more than three months by a breakdown in negotiations between Bing's regime and the orchestra union, as well as the chorus, dancers, and virtually every other union associated with the Met. Bing's somewhat Prussian tactics included a lock-out situation, in which the season was postponed week by week, even though a strike was never actually called. The season was scheduled to begin on September 15. Bing guaranteed the fees of a select group of singers—Tebaldi, Tucker, Corelli, Nilsson, et al.—for the first two months, thereby assuring their presence if the season were to be given after all. When the situation had not improved by mid-November, Bing could no longer continue to pay even his top singers for cancelled performances, and things looked grim. Finally, the week before Christmas, a settlement was reached and the season was scheduled to begin on December 29 with *Aida,* starring Leontyne Price.

Although a number of singers had been reluctantly forced to make other plans, Tebaldi elected to remain available. Thus she was in New York to sing *Tosca* on New Year's Eve, three nights into the season. In fact, Tebaldi had made one appearance in New York that season. A benefit for the musicians was arranged at Philharmonic Hall, and various Met soloists were invited to participate. While a number refused, fearing possible reprisals from Rudolf Bing, Tebaldi and Richard Tucker demonstrated their support of the musicians and concern for their welfare by singing a stirring performance of the fourth act duet from *Andrea Chenier.* In addition to the high quality work from Tebaldi, Konya (Mario) and MacNeil (Scarpia), the New Year's Eve *Tosca* was made memorable by something that did *not* happen: Tosca did not leap to her "death" that night at the end of the third act. Instead, after crying "Scarpia avanti a Dio!", she ran up to the top of the set, then drew back and remained motionless while the startled choristers representing the soldiers gathered round and hid her from view. What had happened to make Tebaldi change Puccini's ending? Backstage, she explained. The stage elevator, which holds the mattress onto which all Toscas jump in order to break their falls, was not raised. Somebody had carelessly left the elevator far below stage level. Treating the matter as lightly as possible, Tebaldi told those of us assembled that "If Rudolf Bing thinks that I'm going to jump fifty feet in the pitch dark for him he's crazy." When she repeated Tosca the following Saturday night, the mattress was in place, and she was able to end the opera in its usual way. She sang also *Tosca* on the broadcast performance—one of the three Puccini works that she broadcast in the sixteen-week season.

Her next broadcast was *La Bohème,* a performance in which Richard Tucker was feted on the occasion of the twenty-fifth anniversary of his American debut. Tucker had specifically asked the Met management to schedule Tebaldi to sing with him that day, as they had maintained the friendliest of relationships over the years and had often sung together. The opera originally scheduled to be broadcast that day was *Andrea Chenier,* but the wholesale changes in scheduling that were the aftermath of the labor dispute necessitated the change.

The most interesting role of Tebaldi's New York season was Minnie, Puccini's *Girl of the Golden West.* Although she had always been scheduled to sing some of the performances of this opera, the premiere was to have been sung by the late Marie Collier. Again, owing to the shortened season, Collier wasn't available when the opera was rescheduled, and so Tebaldi's first Metropolitan Minnie took place at the season's first *Fanciulla.*

Although, as the recording and the Radio Italiana broadcast had already proven, Tebaldi was both vocally and temperamentally well suited to the role of Minnie, singing the role in a fully staged version of the opera presented her with a problem: Minnie has to make her climactic third act entrance on horseback, and Tebaldi has had a lifelong fear of horses. It seems that while her mother was pregnant, she was frightened and nearly run down by a crazed horse. For the rest of Signora Tebaldi's life, she feared and despised horses, and the phobia was inculcated into her daughter from earliest childhood. Therefore, Renata inquired if she might forego Minnie's usual entrance in act three and merely be seen running on. She was not to have her way!

Tebaldi recalls that the stage director, Patrick Tavernia, spoke to her, reminding her that part of the tradition that had grown up around *La Fanciulla del West* was that Minnie, the tough saloon hostess (with the purest heart imaginable), was expected to ride on stage demanding that her lover, Dick Johnson, be set free by the lynch mob. Not to ride the horse, according to Tavernia, would be unthinkable, akin to appearing without a "Western" costume. Thus the soprano was persuaded. Her mind was also set at ease when she saw that the horse in question was an older beast, proven gentle and mild-tempered in his many stage appearances in this and other operas. Someone present at Tebaldi's first rehearsal with the animal recalls that she approached him, patted his mane, and said, "Well, Mr. Horse, I am Tebaldi, you and I are going to be friends, eh?"

If Tebaldi never quite conquered her nervousness about riding Minnie's horse, she at least was able to present a handsome figure in the saddle when the performances were given. Extra time was found at rehearsals for Tebaldi and her mount to practice—the singer laughingly remembers being handed a rehearsal schedule one day that read: "11 A.M. Main Stage, Horse and Madame Tebaldi." One concession that Tebaldi won was to postpone her equestrian entry until the last possible moment, thereby keeping her time astride the beast to the absolute minimum. The horse, however, had other ideas; at every performance he would dash for the stage as soon as he heard the music to which he had formerly galloped into public view, and the stagehands had to restrain him until the new moment for his appearance came.

Horse or not, *Fanciulla* was welcomed by the audience and most of the critics on the evening of February 4, 1970. Although Renata's highest notes that evening, and at several of the later performances, were strident, most of her singing was warm, rich, and under full control. Having lost some weight that year, Tebaldi looked particularly well in her costumes, and she threw herself into the spirit of the melodramatic plot, struggling with Rance with all the vehemence of a Tosca or a Gioconda, but also revealing a flair for comedy, as when Minnie hurriedly runs across the stage in her bloomers, preparing for Johnson's visit to her cabin. Although she denies any previous experience as a player of poker, Tebaldi also managed somehow to deal her game with Rance as if she were a riverboat gambler!

Writing of the opening performance in the *New York Times,* Harold C. Schonberg noted that "It was not so much the way she sang Minnie as the way she acted it that intrigued the buffs. Miss Tebaldi has been singing very much the same way for the last few years—making a very big sound, saving herself for the climaxes. There is a good deal of steel in her voice these days—a hard, burnished sound that has a good deal of authority and relatively little color. At that, she found the role of Minnie vocally congenial once she settled down. She went through the demanding second act with no hint of strain or unease.

"And she, quite literally, in spots, threw herself into the role. She made the official Metropolitan entrance (not Puccini's), shooting the revolver from Sonora's hand, and then proceeded to deliver the primmest, sweetest, most innocent portrait of Minnie that the Metropolitan Opera has ever had. There was temperament to her work, too, but the prevailing impression was of a very feminine, ladylike Minnie of no great brains but infinite love and loyalty. Which is precisely what Puccini intended. The strip-tease down to bloomers and corset, anyway, pleased everybody. Miss Tebaldi did this in a breathless, fluttery sort of way. But that was as nothing against the famous poker game. How deftly she stashed the aces-full hand in her garter! What a pretty leg! . . . With what a gesture of triumph did she hurl the deck in the air as the baffled sheriff left. In the last act Miss Tebaldi made her entrance mounted upon a horse. She and the horse were carefully propped up by supers, but it was the spirit that counted. Yes, it was an adorable portrait and it sent everybody home happy."

Fausto Cleva conducted the opera, and at the first performance Tebaldi's principal colleagues included Sandor Konya (suffering from a bad cold) as Dick Johnson and Giangiacomo Guelfi as Rance. At subsequent performances, Colzani sang Rance, a role he had been singing with the Metropolitan since *Fanciulla's* first Bing-era revival in 1961. It was grand watching Tebaldi and Colzani, two Italian singers who had faced each other so often as Tosca and Scarpia, fighting a similar battle in western garb. Perhaps the aura of happiness that settled over these *Fanciulla* performances had as much to do with the tear-jerking but happy ending of the work (never before had Tebaldi been left alive at final curtain, except in *Boccanegra* when Amelia is left grief-stricken at the Doge's murder!) as it did with the quality of Tebaldi's singing. For whatever reason, the New York public was delighted by the production and Tebaldi received some of the longer, more frantic ovations of her career.

After her *Fanciulla* on March 14, Tebaldi sang no more that season. She did, however, find herself in the newspapers on June 3, the day after she testified in a court case involving a tax accountant, Norman H. Egenberg. It seems that Egenberg, who prepared the tax returns of a number of the Metropolitan's foreign artists, including Tebaldi, Corelli, Konya, Vickers, Freni, and others, had been falsifying returns quite wildly, and without the knowledge of the artists.

In Tebaldi's case, the accountant had stated that she paid more than $2,000 each year for a claque. Moreover, he had stated that Renata did not plan to return to the United States. She, like her colleagues who had engaged Egenberg to help them with the difficult-to-understand U.S. tax forms, had signed her returns without reading them. Thus, when the prosecuting attorney asked her if it were true that she had paid a claque, she replied, "I have never paid a claque in my life!" She also denied that she was leaving the States, never to return. The case ended with Tebaldi and the other clients completely exonerated, but Egenberg was convicted and sent to prison.

After spending the summer in Europe, where she recorded Verdi's *Un Ballo in maschera*, the soprano returned to New York in time for the 1970-71 season's first *Andrea Chenier* on October 9, a performance conducted by Cleva with Carlo Bergonzi as Chenier and Colzani as Gerard. The *Chenier* performances of this season represent Tebaldi's most troubled time at the Metropolitan. Although she looked well, and manifested the best of spirits, something was clearly affecting her singing. The middle range, particularly when she sang softly, was as fresh as ever. High notes, however, were becoming difficult. Of the nine performances, only four can really be said to have gone well for her. The situation seemed to reach a crisis on the evening of December 23, when Tebaldi, though suffering from the flu and running a temperature, gallantly elected to sing so as not to disappoint the audience. While many singers request that an announcement be made when they are singing with a cold or other ailment, Renata chose to say nothing to anyone.

Short of a disaster such as that which befell Leonard Warren, there is nothing more horrifying for an audience than to watch an artist sing while ill. As the effects of Tebaldi's bout with influenza became more apparent, the audience listened with increasing concern. The love duet in the second act did not go at all well. The audience was enormously sympathetic—it need not be stated at this point that Renata Tebaldi is a great favorite of the Metropolitan public. Following the aria "La mamma morta" in the third act, many people began to shout "brava" even though the singing fell far short of her usual standard. Tebaldi, however, cut the applause short by shaking her heard and saying "I am sorry" softly but audibly to those in the front of the house. The intermission which followed the third act lasted twice as long as usual, and before the fourth act started an assistant stage manager did speak to the audience, saying that Tebaldi had the flu but would finish the performance. Fortunately, even with the strenuous final duet, the fourth act went considerably better, and many in the audience remained to shower praise on Tebaldi and her colleagues (who that night included Domingo in the title role). Five days remained before the next *Chenier*, which was also Tebaldi's final performance that season. Throughout those five days, the Tebaldiani worried, hoped, wrote her letters of encouragement. By the evening of December 28, the Metropolitan "regulars" were highly keyed up, and many of Tebaldi's New York admirers entered the opera house in a state of trepidation. How deeply Tebaldi herself must have been aware of this tension! Her keen professionalism was evident as she arrived at the stage door on time, and she proceeded to make up for the role in spite of having accidentally jammed her finger in the door of her automobile as she stepped out at the stage door. The performance began with Domingo again singing Chenier and with Cornell MacNeil singing Gerard for the first time that season.

It was difficult to tell anything of Tebaldi's vocal condition during the first act, as Maddalena has little to sing. However, the great duet in the second act went far better than it had five days before. Realizing this herself, Tebaldi gained in confidence, and delivered a searing rendition of "La mamma morta" which had the audience cheering. The upward trend continued and the evening ended in triumph for Tebaldi. Her singing that evening seemed freer of constriction in the upper register than it had at any time that season. Many phrases were caressed by her voice almost as of old, and the entire evening had the masterful stamp of a Tebaldi performance upon it! Tebaldi left the Met that night justifiably pleased with her own work, and overwhelmed by the ovation she received at the end of the opera.

The following week, before leaving for Italy, Tebaldi returned to Philadelphia to sing a Desdemona with the Philadelphia Lyric Opera, in the company of Jon Vickers as Otello and Peter Glossop as Iago. Anton Guadagno conducted. Desdemona is one of the most vocally congenial of Tebaldi's roles, and the performance went well. This *Otello* performance was

Tebaldi's first since 1967, (at Newport, Rhode Island), and one was struck by the intensified dramatic involvement of her Desdemona, particularly in the third act, where Tebaldi now manifested greater fire in her reactions to the Moor's hysterical accusations than ever before. Jon Vickers, an eloquent and powerful Otello, worked well with Tebaldi, and the performance had many moments of brilliant excitement. Vocally, too, Tebaldi was in fine condition, and her customary elegance in phrasing this music was undiminished. Backstage that evening, Tebaldi mentioned that her Metropolitan commitments for the following season included *Tosca* and her first Metropolitan performances of the role of Mistress Alice Ford in *Falstaff.* The role had been one of Tebaldi's successes at La Scala and the San Carlo Opera of Naples. She had also sung the role in a marvelous 1958 revival at the Chicago Lyric Opera with Tito Gobbi as Falstaff, Rolando Panerai as Ford, Anna Moffo as Nanette, and Giulietta Simionato as Dame Quickly, with Tullio Serafin conducting. Thus the 1971-72 Metropolitan season—which, incidentally, was to be Sir Rudolf Bing's last as general manager—promised much.

However, Tebaldi was not to make her next public appearance for thirteen months, during which time some important changes were to occur. Despite the success of the last two performances of her 1970-71 season, the final *Chenier* at the Met and the Philadelphia *Otello,* Tebaldi realized that her singing of late had been uneven. Giving this a great deal of thought, the soprano realized that, as had happened eight years earlier, some defects in technique were becoming apparent. Therefore she returned to Italy and began painstakingly to restudy her art in preparation for the new season. She was determined to eliminate the flaws in her singing, concentrating on lightening her tone, strengthening her high notes, and eliminating the need to sing her top notes with her head down, as if forcing the tones from her throat.

Tebaldi also discontinued studying with Ugo de Caro, who, although he had helped her recover from her 1963 vocal crisis, had failed her in 1970 by not aiding her to change her method of vocal production when new problems developed.

Thus Tebaldi labored deeply and by herself throughout 1971 to regain command of her voice. By early October, she decided to forego her five scheduled Toscas at the Metropolitan, which were to be sung during November, and concentrate on preparing Mistress Alice Ford for the *Falstaff* revival, which would begin in late February and last until April 1. In addition, Tebaldi accepted the role of Desdemona in the Met's spring tour and further performances of that role as well as *Falstaff* in Bing's final June Festival, which was to be devoted to the works of Bing's favorite composer, Verdi.

The cancellation of the five *Tosca* performances represented the first Metropolitan cancellations by Tebaldi since 1963. Although her Metropolitan public was sorely disappointed by the news that she would not sing the Puccini work (Grace Bumbry and Dorothy Kirsten took over the performances), spirits were buoyed by the fact that Tebaldi was still scheduled for *Falstaff*.

Tebaldi arrived in New York in January and immediately commenced rehearsals for the Verdi comedy—the first comic work she had ever performed at the Metropolitan. She also began to be seen attending Metropolitan performances. On the night of her birthday, February 1, Tebaldi attended the Metropolitan's first *Werther* of the season, which starred Corelli and Regine Crespin. Resplendently dressed, Tebaldi received ovations from the audience as she swept down the aisle in the Orchestra section of the Met, and she was mobbed by fans at each intermission. A description of Renata Tebaldi's first performance of *Falstaff* on February 25, 1972 served to open this book. In all, there were seven *Falstaffs*, and all of them were cordially received by Met audiences. Tebaldi's year of restudying had paid off well—she had greatly lightened her voice, and had little if any difficulty with top notes, rising easily to the B flat called for in the second act cry "Misericordia," and ending each performance with a joyously firm high C held for nine beats.

Furthermore, Tebaldi's sense of comedy, previously confined to a few minutes in the second acts of *La Bohème* and *Fanciulla*, was now revealed for an entire opera! This Mistress Ford was also a mistress of the quick, witty physical reaction and a sure hand at onstage merrymaking. Watching Tebaldi arch an eyebrow while reading Falstaff's "letter of introduction," or noting her bemused expression when Falstaff replaced Alice's handsome vase of flowers with a scraggly posy of his own was a joy! Tebaldi looked well and moved gracefully in the Zeffirelli production, and she contributed to a sense of ensemble in the singing and the acting.

Her colleagues, in general, were of high calibre, although after the first performance Sir Geraint Evans seemed to lose interest in the role of Falstaff; at each of his four remaining performances he demonstrated less and less feeling for either the words or the music. He was replaced on March 27 by Tito Gobbi, who sang Falstaff twice, including the broadcast performance of April 1. Incredibly, Gobbi had not sung with Tebaldi at the Met since the *Tosca* of March 1964. Their *Falstaff* performances were viewed with special nostalgia by members of the audience who recalled those performances, or who had seen the two together in Europe or Chicago, where they had sung *Falstaff* in the memorable 1958 revival and those especially blessed *Adriana* performances shortly before the death of Tebaldi's mother, in casts that also included Di Stefano and Simionato, with Serafin conducting. Falstaff and Mistress Alice have only a few moments in the second act in which they really work together, but Gobbi and Tebaldi made the most of their short rendezvous, giving this wonderful scene a special glow. While Tebaldi's singing at the first performance of *Falstaff* was in every sense worthy of her, each repeat performance found her in even better form. More than one observer familiar with past performances of the Verdi comedy in other revivals of the current production, as well as revivals of two or more decades earlier, declared that she was the finest Alice Ford in their Metropolitan experience.

As spring arrived, the details of the gala concert that would conclude the regular season and commemorate the end of Bing's twenty-two years as general manager were made public. Virtually every major artist on the current Met roster was invited to sing. Tebaldi was to join Franco Corelli, her partner on so many occasions at both the old and new Metropolitan opera houses, in the love duet "Già nella notte densa" from the first act of *Otello.* This would be the tenor's first performance of any music from *Otello* in public (he had recorded the "Esultate" for Cetra Records at the beginning of his career) and naturally the fans were eager to hear Franco and Renata sing together once again.

There had been a great deal of interest in the Bing gala—including a near riot in the early hours of the Sunday morning on which the standing room tickets were to have gone on sale, owing to some latecomers "crashing" the line that had formed the previous afternoon. (As a face-saving gesture, the standing room places were yanked from sale that day and distributed by Bing himself to winners of a lottery held inside the opera house the following Sunday morning.) Much disappointment was expressed, however, when it became known two days before the concert that Tebaldi had taken ill and could not appear. Thus Tebaldi, whom Bing had called "the finest singer he had brought to the Met" in a *Newsweek* interview published the week of the concert, did not even receive a place on the program.

Tebaldi was also supposed to open the annual Metropolitan spring tour in Boston the Monday after the Bing gala. However, her illness, which involved muscular spasms in her neck, was slow to improve. She was thus forced to cancel that performance, and, within a few days, the rest of the tour and even the four performances scheduled for the Metropolitan in the June Verdi Festival. Tebaldi, whose reluctance to break a contract had become almost legendary, was thus forced to cancel more than half of her scheduled Metropolitan commitments in the 1971-72 season. She was heard that spring in a special, two-hour interview broadcast on WNYC-FM, in which she reviewed her career with host John Charles Miller. This program, which was recorded in March, proved highly popular, and was repeated twice within the next six months.

The Met was preparing for an ambitious season under the new leadership of Goeran Gentele. The new Swedish manager had just completed successful negotiations with the various labor unions, to insure three more seasons without a strike when the shocking news of his death in an auto crash in Sardinia was announced. Gentele who had demonstrated an understanding of the problems faced by the Met, as well as a wealth of new ideas for the future, died barely eighteen days after officially taking over from Sir Rudolf Bing!

The stunned board of directors appointed Schuyler G. Chapin, who had been designated as Gentele's assistant, as interim general manager, making his appointment permanent a few months later.

Tebaldi, who had met with Gentele the previous winter and signed a contract for a brief (one-week) engagement in January, during which she would sing Desdemona three times, had decided to occupy herself with an ambitious, coast-to-coast concert tour. Beginning in December, she and Franco Corelli, with Geoffrey Parsons at the piano, were to sing in several major American cities. After a break during which she would fulfill her Metropolitan contract in *Otello*, Tebaldi would make a solo tour of fifteen U.S. and Canadian cities. Tebaldi had often sung concerts in the States at the beginning of her Met career, including a celebrated appearance at Carnegie Hall in 1957, and had since sung in many U.S. cities large and small. However, in recent years, she had concentrated almost solely on operatic appearances with the Metropolitan. While the Met's spring tours brought her to such cities as Boston, Atlanta, Cleveland, and Dallas, and she had occasionally sung with regional operas in Boston, Cleveland, and Hartford, there were many cities in which she had not appeared in a decade or more. Thus a concert tour was arranged under the auspices of Columbia Artists Management.

During the summer of 1972, Tebaldi worked with conductor Richard Bonynge, the bel canto specialist and husband of Joan Sutherland, and prepared a program of Italian songs written between the seventeenth and twentieth centuries. She recorded a number of these with Bonynge at the piano and these were released by London to coincide with her concert tour.

For the concerts that she was singing with Corelli, each artist was to sing sets consisting of two pieces, and each half of the concert would be closed by a duet from a Puccini opera—"O soave fanciulla" from *Bohème* ended the first part, while the duet from the first act of *Tosca* (from "Chi è quella donna bionda lassù?) would close the concert. The tour began in New Orleans, and included concerts in Nashville, Washington, and Philadelphia. Tebaldi acquired a stunning collection of concert gowns, which she alternated at each concert. At her solo evening on April 1, she favored the New York audience with a new dress for the second half.

The program itself was on the light side, disappointing those who had hoped for an evening totally devoted to operatic excerpts. The songs, which included such well-known pieces as "Ah cessate di piagarmi," "M'ha preso all sua ragna," Rossini's "La regata veneziana," and Verdi's "Stornello," also featured less well-known songs by such operatic composers as Verdi, Ponchielli, Zandonai, Mascagni, and Puccini.

Tebaldi demonstrated a warm, rather intimate concert style, singing directly to her audience, occasionally seeming to address individual phrases to people whom she recognized, and imbuing each piece with a specific character, as if creating a mini-drama (or comedy) with each number. She later confirmed to me that she worked very hard at creating a specific, suitable mood and sense of character for every song in her repertoire. After the *Tosca* duet, Tebaldi always sang at least one and occasionally two encores, usually "Non ti scordare di me" or "A Vuchella." Audiences were invariably enthusiastic, judging from the warm applause and the many curtain calls that both Tebaldi and Corelli drew.

Typically, Tebaldi's dressing room was filled with hundreds of admirers who lingered after each concert, many of whom had waited literally years to hear her. Tebaldi remained seated, tirelessly accepting greetings, making small talk, and signing autographs, often for as long as ninety minutes after a concert had ended. Tebaldi's generosity with her time surprised and even irked custodians at some theatres, who wanted to close up and go home. Tebaldi however, never left until the last fan, new or old friend, had been properly greeted.

She was particularly touched by the presence backstage of a large number of young people, many of whom were hearing her live for the first time at these concerts but who had "grown up" with her recordings and Metropolitan broadcasts.

Tebaldi arrived back in New York in late December to prepare for her first Met Desdemona in eight years, and her very first in the new *Otello* productions designed and directed by Franco Zeffirelli, unveiled the previous March as the last new production of the Bing era.

On the evening of January 2, a crowd at least as large as that which habitually welcomed Tebaldi upon her return each season met in front of the stage door shortly before seven o'clock. Excitement was high, for Desdemona was, to be sure, one of Tebaldi's best roles. The familiar "ritual" of waiting for the limousine to arrive, the greeting of the diva, and the killing of the final hour before the performance was faithfully followed; then, at last, the new year's first performance of *Otello* began. James Levine conducted, James McCracken was singing the Moor, and Sherrill Milnes took the role of Iago.

Tebaldi made her entrance at the top of a large flight of "stone" steps, looking especially radiant in a pale blue gown, with a comely long blond wig flowing down her shoulders. Although she experienced a moment's unsteadiness of intonation as she began to sing, Tebaldi soon warmed to the music and her singing began to take on much of the assurance of former days. Her performance of the brutal confrontation with Otello in the third act, "Dio ti giocondi, o sposo" was exceptionally powerful. Tebaldi was singing with the intensity and sensitivity which she customarily brought to Desdemona, although at that first performance she was hampered by lack of stage rehearsal, and often thought it best to make her dramatic points by standing still. The brilliant ensemble which caps the third act went well that evening, as did the "Willow Song" and "Ave Maria." Tebaldi conveyed Desdemona's terror more vividly than ever that evening, and retained her composure even when McCracken, a big, powerful man, nearly pushed her off Desdemona's high, narrow bed in a moment of seemingly un-

Tebaldi as Mimi in *La Bohème*
(photo by Louis Melançon).

Tebaldi as Violetta in *La Traviata*
at the Metropolitan Opera in 1957 (Melançon).

Tebaldi as Aïda.

With the author in the green room of the Philadelphia Academy of Music after a recital on December 20, 1972.

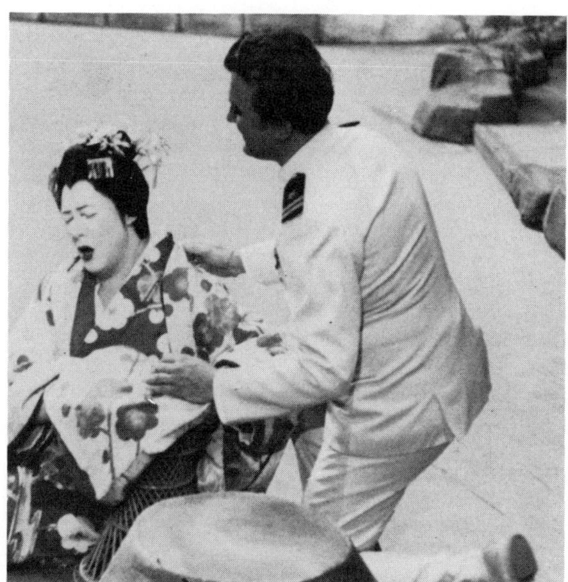

A scene from Act One of a Metropolitan Opera performance of *Madama Butterfly,* with Nicolai Gedda.

A happy moment in Act Two of *La Bohème* when Tebaldi returned to the Metropolitan on March 14, 1964.

Sharing a curtain call with Carlo Bergonzi and Sherill Milnes after a 1966 Met performance of *Andrea Chenier.*

The soprano receives an honorary degree at Villanova University in 1966.

"Ciao, Mr. New."

With Franco Corelli, Tebaldi sang an excerpt from *Manon Lescaut* at the gala closing of the old Metropolitan Opera House on April 16, 1966.

A happy Tebaldi takes a bow after a performance of *La Gioconda* at the Met in 1966.

Above left: Tebaldi as Mistress Ford in *Falstaff* pretends to flirt with Tito Gobbi's Sir John; from the Teatro San Carlo, Naples, 1962. Above: Tebaldi as Alice Ford at the Chicago Lyric Opera in 1958. Right: Tebaldi and Del Monaco in a scene from Act Three of *Otello* at the Metropolitan in 1955 (Melançon). Far right: Tebaldi as Giordano's Fedora at La Scala.

Smiling backstage following a 1966 dress rehearsal of *Adriana Lecouvreur* at the Met.

With Corelli following *La Bohème* at the Metropolitan in June of 1966.

Left: A jubilant Tebaldi points her pistol at the audience following *La Fanciulla del West* at the Met in 1970. Below left: Backstage, dressed as Minnie. Below right: Leaving the Met following a performance of *Andrea Chenier* in 1970.

Tebaldi in an emotional moment from Act Three of *Andrea Chenier;* from La Scala, 1962.

Tebaldi as Puccini's Manon at the Metropolitan Opera in 1958 (Melançon).

Tebaldi (with George London as Baron Scarpia) in *Tosca* at the Met in 1958 (Melançon).

Tebaldi as Tosca at the Paris Opera.

controlled murderous passion. Following the performance, the entire audience rose to its feet, and lavished one of the warmest ovations yet seen at the new Met upon Tebaldi, who stood before the curtain with tears of happiness streaming down her face, waving in her familiar manner, both hands outstretched, crying "I love you" over and over again.

Three nights later, as one observer sadly remarked, Tebaldi completed the second third of her entire Met season, with a Desdemona that had clearly gained from familiarity with the production. Obviously learning the staging from that one performance, Tebaldi's physical acting was more vivid than it had been the previous Tuesday, while her singing, even with some steely high notes, had taken on even more security of production, and there was only one moment, in the fourth act, when she sang off-pitch.

The following Monday Tebaldi sang what has been to date her last appearance at the Met. The date, January 8, was just three weeks short of the eighteenth anniversary of her Metropolitan debut. The performance was in no sense a farewell, yet it had a real air of poignancy about it.

Tebaldi's final bows of the season were greeted ecstatically by the loyal Metropolitan audience. After the opera, the management granted Tebaldi a rare concession—while artists were usually permitted only six personal visitors backstage, she was told that as many of her fans as she wanted could come backstage. Knowing friends among the audience were waiting outside the stage door, Tebaldi, assisted by Tina, prepared a list. My own name was at the top of that list, and you may well imagine my surprise when one of the Metropolitan's uniformed policemen appeared at the stage door and began shouting for me to identify myself. I did so, and was astonished and nonplussed to be gruffly told that I was wanted inside. For a mad moment I decided it had been discovered that back in 1967 I had bribed a doorman to let me attend a sold-out *Gioconda* performance without a ticket, and I half expected to be formally banned from future attendance at the Met! Instead, I was marched to the entrance of the Green Room, where artists receive their guests if they choose not to entertain them in the dressing room area. I was told that Mme. Tebaldi would see me now! There, in the Green Room, Renata Tebaldi spent nearly an hour reminiscing with people who had assembled. We spoke of other nights, of triumphs, of the time when the horse received billing over Tebaldi on a *Fanciulla del West* rehearsal schedule sheet. At one point, Tebaldi, near tears, suddenly asked everyone to remain silent for a moment. The mood passed, and Tebaldi began to talk of her coming concert tour, which was to commence six weeks later on the West Coast. Then people still had photos and programs for Tebaldi to sign. Tebaldi's patience at this task of autographing seemingly endless stacks of playbills, old concert programs, and photos is as inexhaustible as the material handed her. Lois Kirschenbaum, the "Dean" of New York's opera fans, carries two bags filled with candids (a number of which are reproduced in this book), publicity pictures, schedules, etcetera; as one of the most dedicated of Tebaldi's fans, she was also invited backstage, and presented the diva with still more pictorial mementos to autograph. Lois and I have traveled together on many occasions, returning from Philadelphia and other operatic centers of interest, often serenading Greyhound bus passengers with playbacks of performances. The ebullient, energetic Miss Kirschenbaum had attended virtually all of Tebaldi's New York area performances since the late 1950s and she, like all present, felt the special wistfulness of the occasion. No one wanted to put these feelings into words, but everyone present wondered when the next time might be that Renata Tebaldi would greet them backstage at the Metropolitan Opera. Finally, a few minutes before 1 A.M., Tebaldi felt that it was time to leave. Tina and I carried a few of her belongings out to the car, while New, her little grey poodle, walked jauntily behind us. There were still people outside waiting to say goodnight to the diva, and she bid them each good-bye for the present. As the sleek Cadillac sped away, more than one person wondered if an era had just ended.

Tebaldi continued her concert tour, singing to packed houses around the United States. Her Carnegie Hall concert was scheduled for April 1. The driving rain which fell all day long meant that there were few people waiting outside the unprotected Carnegie Hall stage entrance, but a capacity crowd filled the famous concert hall. The solo program included many of the songs that Tebaldi had been performing in tandem with Corelli, as well as new pieces. Beethoven's concert aria "Ah, perfido" now began the second half of the program, and Mascagni's aria "Flammen, perdonami" from *Lodoletta* was also scheduled. At the New York concert, as in all of the other half-dozen that I managed to attend, this piece brought down the house. Tebaldi ended the concert with two light, charming songs by Buzzi-Pescia, the "Serenata Spagnola" and the "Serenata Veneziana." After these two pieces the applause was deafening. Flowers were presented by ushers and thrown to the stage from all corners of the house by fans! The encores came: "O mio babbino caro," "Non ti scordar di me," "If I Loved You," which drew a happy roar of recognition from the crowd, and "A Vuchella." The cheering went on for nearly forty-five minutes after the concert ended, as the spectators poured out a loving tribute. It was an emotional, happy evening for all concerned. As always, the backstage scene was mobbed with scores of people pressing their way up the narrow staircase, eager to congratulate Tebaldi personally. She herself seemed cheerful, and looked radiant in her salmon-colored gown. Although this was undoubtedly the most exciting concert, it was not the last one. Five nights later Tebaldi repeated the program in Ottawa, and Philadelphia and New Haven, among other locations, were still to come.

Before flying to Italy for summer vacation, Tebaldi teamed with Corelli for a pair of operatic concerts, with full orchestra, in Cincinnati and Philadelphia. At these, she sang "Ritorna vincitor," "Deh vieni non tardar," and an especially exciting "Voi lo sapete," which was so thrilling that one was sad Tebaldi still hadn't appeared in a fully staged *Cavalleria Rusticana*.

Early in the fall, Tebaldi and Corelli sang concerts in London and Vienna. Tebaldi hadn't appeared in London for eighteen years, but people who remembered her Covent Garden appearances in *Tosca* and knew her from recordings queued up to wait for her at the artists' entrance of the Royal Albert Hall. By a coincidence, the concert was scheduled less than two weeks after the cancellation of a Maria Callas–Giuseppe di Stefano concert, which was to have been Callas's return to public activity after an eight-year absence. The London press played up the old rivalry, and, on the afternoon before the concert, one paper published an interview with Tebaldi under the headline "OPERA RIVAL SINGS WHILE MARIA WAITS!"

The London Audience that packed Albert Hall on October 9 was treated to one of Tebaldi's best evenings in recent years. Her program included many of the pieces which she had been singing throughout the United States, and if, as in America, some were disappointed that the program contained few operatic selections, the singing itself was highly applauded, especially when Tebaldi sang "Voi lo sapete" and, as an encore, "Flammen perdonami." The two Puccini duets that Tebaldi and Corelli customarily sang on these joint recitals were well received, with the *Tosca* duet being especially impressive.

After London, the soprano journeyed to Vienna, and then sang several concerts in the Far East. As this book goes to press, Tebaldi is preparing a second consecutive American concert tour. She says that she enjoys singing concerts, for they bring her very close to the audience. She has proven to be adept as a concert artist too, for, while singing always on a grand scale, Renata Tebaldi addresses her singing to her audience, finding means to create a sense of rapport with her listeners, and never seems at the least disadvantage without the "protective trappings" of costumes, scenery, or a specific character to portray.

As Renata Tebaldi enters 1974, the very mention of her name—or its appearance on a billboard advertising a future appearance—commands respect and attention, and, to millions, an intense admiration and vast affection. Whether she continues to concentrate on concert appearances, or soon returns to the operatic stage in New York, London, and other centers, she can look back upon a career spanning three decades of legion—and legendary—successes. Renata Tebaldi is not a person who worries inordinately about the future—I daresay that she is a great deal more concerned with the immediate present or the recent past than she is with the far-off future. One thing is certain: she will continue to sing with her special qualities of vocal splendor, musicianship, and personal graciousness for years to come, and, when future histories of opera are compiled, she will have a place beside the other fabled great personalities of song.

Tebaldi the Artist

If one were asked to name Renata Tebaldi's finest attribute as a performer, the answer would be, of course, her voice. However greatly her gifts as a musician and actress contribute to her preeminence in her art, the mere sound of her voice, in peak form, is one of the most remarkable musical experiences imaginable.

Tebaldi first impressed listeners, including her early teachers Riccardo Zandonai and Carmen Melis, with her relatively untrained, natural voice when she was an adolescent. Those worthy, sophisticated musicians were in agreement that an instrument like Tebaldi's is created only once or twice each century, and it was this argument that helped persuade Tebaldi's mother to agree to her daughter's vocation as an opera singer. How stirring an experience it must be for a teacher of music to have a young student enter his studio one day, unknown, unheralded, and seemingly no different from the scores of young, would-be artists with whom he is in contact every day, until the unknown begins to sing, revealing a talent as extraordinary as Tebaldi's!

Tebaldi as Tosca at the Vienna State Opera in 1958.

How difficult it is to describe any voice, let alone that of Renata Tebaldi. Adjectives become futile, and writing in this era of the phonograph and the tape recorder, one is tempted merely to suggest that the reader obtain a Tebaldi record and hear for himself! The words commonly used to describe Tebaldi's voice, "Lush," "large," "warm," "ravishing," and so on, hardly convey a true sense of the sound she creates when she sings. Comparisons to other singers aren't very helpful either, for Tebaldi is unique among artists. As with Caruso and Chaliapin, Price and, for that matter, Callas, others will be compared to *her* when something in their work suggests it. One singer to whom Tebaldi has often been compared is the Italian soprano Claudia Muzio. Muzio, who sang from the late 1910s to the 1930s, is said to have shared with Tebaldi a quality which Italians call *morbidezza,* that is, a sense of human frailty, sadness, and mortality. They also shared their repertoire, as Muzio was a celebrated Adriana, Leonora in *Forza* and Tosca (although Muzio also sang Bellini operas). Muzio was a beautiful woman, though one who, far more so than Tebaldi, lived under a shadow of personal despair and tragedy. Yet, judging from records made well before the age of high fidelity, the elder soprano's voice was harder, less rich, and not nearly as beautiful as Tebaldi's. Like Tebaldi, she had superb control of breath and an ability to shape a line, to phrase, that was born and *not* learned.

Tebaldi, while acknowledging that others have found similarities between her voice and Muzio's, insists that she neither heard Muzio in performance nor listened to her records during her artistically formative years. In fact, Tebaldi recalls that as a young girl her family had access to few discs, and, of those she did have, the ones she listened to most often were recordings of coloratura Toti dal Monte, who, except for Cio-cio-san, sang a repertoire completely different from Tebaldi's own! As there is no one else with whom comparisons are completely apt, one must examine Tebaldi's own work, and find therein the standards that she set.

Sir Rudolf Bing, when asked to enumerate the special qualities that, in his estimation, distinguished Tebaldi's singing, spoke of "the fabulous warmth" of her voice, and "her incredible control of volume." Her command of the *piano* and *pianissimo* has always been one of her finest attributes as a singer. For example, listen to Tebaldi, as Aïda, seduce Radames in the Nile Scene on her first *Aïda* recording, now available on Richmond. How grandly and yet how effortlessly she spins out "Là . . . trale foreste vergini," or how sweetly the voice floats up on the last phrase in that section, "Fuggiam, fuggiam!" Then, of course, there is that high B flat "Amen" at the close of Desdemona's "Ave Maria" in Act Four of *Otello*. Either of the commercial recordings, and the tapes of Metropolitan broadcasts (as well as one from Naples in 1952 with Tebaldi, Del Monaco, and Bechi that is worth searching for in pirates' catalogues) reveal her superb handling of this phrase. "Superb" is a word that kept cropping up in conversations with Bing in connection with this book. "Tebaldi was superb in every role she sang when she came to the Met", said the former general manager, who now lectures at Brooklyn College and handles that institution's concert bookings. Bing revealed, however, that he personally did not much care for Tebaldi's Tosca, dismissing this as a vagary of his personal taste.

High notes, of course, are not an end in themselves, and when treated as such become akin to circus stunts. Tebaldi's singing, in fact, has never been geared to superhigh notes. She has rarely, if ever, sung above high C, and certainly no such note can be found on her recordings. Even as early as her monaural recordings for London-Decca, high Cs were often produced with some pressure, providing the only "edge" in a voice remarkable for gossamer smoothness everywhere else. Where Tebaldi always triumphed was in the flow of her voice in the two octaves leading up to high C, and in her instinctive fidelity to the stylistic demands of those composers whose works form the substance of her repertoire: Verdi, Puccini, and the *verismo* composers Giordano, Mascagni, Cilea, and so on.

The very hugeness of her voice left her without the ultimate agility for the fioritura of the Donizetti and Bellini heroines.

This fact almost certainly led Tebaldi to specialize in the later operas of Verdi, and those of his successors, whose music called for voices of great power that could sing long but relatively unembellished melodic lines. The music of Puccini exemplifies this style of composition, and few will question that Tebaldi is the greatest Puccini singer to have appeared thus far in the history of his operas!

Interestingly, Maria Callas, billed by the press and the uninformed as Tebaldi's greatest rival, has always been at her best in operas that call for coloratura virtuosity and stratospheric high notes. Callas's Tosca is undoubtedly a great achievement, but one that made its effect more from her brilliant characterization and acting than from the beauty of her singing. Callas's other Puccini performances on recordings always show highly intelligent characterization and uncommon musicianship, but her Mimi, Manon Lescaut, and Cio-cio-san are colder and more remote vocally than Tebaldi's. Again, the two were not rivals at all; the key achievements of the American soprano's career were in such roles as Medea, Lucia, Elvira in *Puritani*, Norma, and Amina, none of which Tebaldi sang. Tebaldi, on the other hand, triumphed in the Puccini operas, which, except for *Tosca,* Callas rarely sang, and in the opinion of many her greatest role is Desdemona, which Callas never sang on stage.

Tebaldi has always seemed most comfortable when singing at slow tempi. Her singing of Verdi's "Stornello" on the early song recital disk finds that piece taken at a considerably slower speed than is customary—in her 1973 concerts, she sang it at a rather brisker pace. This fondness for gentle tempi allowed her to emphasize what was best in her singing—the emotionally rapt crescendo in that haunting midsection from "Mi chiamono Mimi," for example—and enabled her to create her characterizations through detailed realization of the music. Since there is no single technique in the world that is perfect in all situations, and no one style of singing that is equally suited to all styles of composition, there are moments in some of Tebaldi's roles that suit her less well than others. In addition to the "Sempre libera" section of Violetta's first act *scena* (about which so much has been written that the very real beauty of Tebaldi's *Traviata* has nearly been obscured), some of the more florid passages of Leonora on the *Trovatore* recording came heavily to her.

In recent years, there has also been a tendency on the soprano's part to use her chest register more and more frequently for dramatic emphasis. This vividness of vocal coloration has struck some as odd, given the seamlessness of virtually all of Tebaldi's singing in roughly the first two decades of her career. The "chestiness" of some of the *Gioconda* performances, and even some of the later *Cheniers* and *Toscas*, seems to me the result of Tebaldi's ever-growing dramatic awareness, which led her to change and experiment constantly, as well as the inevitable changes in the voice that occurred after thirty years of singing.

At this point, it will be obvious that my own personal taste places me squarely among the most dedicated admirers of Renata Tebaldi. But even given these sympathies, it seems equally apparent that to dwell on the flaws in Tebaldi's singing is to carp unduly, and, furthermore, to be ungrateful to the vocal gifts that she has lavished on audiences since her debut. If there is a voice that soars more wondrously in the roles of Mimi or Cio-cio-san, I do not know it. One doubts if the torment of Desdemona or the passions of Maddalena have ever been expressed more poignantly or with more glorious sound.

Tebaldi's Tosca is certainly one of the two great ones of the current era, the other one being that of Maria Callas. Originally, the two interpretations were diametrically opposed, with Tebaldi emphasizing the gentle side of Tosca's nature, making her truly a woman who had lived for love. In later years, Tebaldi's Tosca began to manifest more of the dramatic ferocity formerly associated only with Callas's portrayal of the Puccini heroine. By 1970, the most recent series of *Toscas* that Tebaldi has sung, her Floria Tosca clearly had a double-edged personality—kittenishly affectionate to Mario, but savagely effective in dealing with Scarpia.

Tebaldi's view of Tosca at this time is very definitely that of a powerful and volatile personality! "Tosca is a strong woman.

She has no difficulty in reaching the decision to murder Scarpia when she realizes that there is no other way to save Mario Cavarodossi. Tosca never weeps, except at the end of the first act when Scarpia has managed to convince her that Cavarodossi has been unfaithful to her. You see, Tosca is so sure of herself as a woman that until that time it has never even occurred to her that she could have a rival in love."

Listening to either of her commercial recordings of *Tosca* and then playing a tape of a more recent Metropolitan performance reveals a startlingly increased emphasis on the melodramatic aspects of her role. Lines such as "Assassino, voglio vederlo," and "E avanti a lui tremava tutta Roma" are now spoken with the most chilling disdain.

Many of the reviews quoted earlier document the reaction to the sound of Tebaldi's voice. During her peak years of singing, it seemed inconceivable that this voice could ever produce less than a totally beautiful note. It is a tribute to Tebaldi's artistry that her performances remained compelling even after the passage of time robbed her of her greatest nights of singing. For, in addition to the majesty of her vocal endowment, a key element of Tebaldi's art has always been one that transcended even the peerless music that she made humanity. Renata Tebaldi's singing always touched the heart. Opera being a hybrid of music and drama, the greatest operatic performers are those who create theatre as well as song. The artistry of such a singer as Tebaldi reveals an awareness of the drama of her roles, and much of her success lies in her ability to communicate character as well as music.

Operatic acting is, obviously, very different from acting in the spoken theatre. The operatic artist, unlike his counterpart in nonmusical drama, is vastly aided by the composer in the expression of mood or emotion. The fact that, say, Aida's sadness is expressed in the music of "O patria mia" does not mean that the soprano performing that role can stand back and merely hit the notes correctly. Verdi's music gives the words a further dimension of meaning, and the combination is such that the listener is doubly affected. It goes almost without saying that great music gives mediocre texts a dignity and validity that the words alone would lack. Operatic acting does not have to be physically busy. An artist standing motionless on stage who infuses every word and note with deep understanding can be far more effective than one who lurches busily about the stage paying little attention to the meaning of the text.

There have been many renowned singers who have been content simply to stand out there on stage and sing, confident that the mere sound of their voice would carry them through the performance. However, I submit that the very finest of singers have always been those who worked on characterization and emotional expression even when sheer beauty of their song would have enabled them to find favor with their public.

Renata Tebaldi is an artist whose skill at characterization has deepened as her career progressed. Her ability to give expression to various emotions has become more pronounced over the years, but on the evidence of recordings and tapes Tebaldi has always been interested in the drama of each of the operas in which she has sung, even in the days when her mode of expression was far more reserved than it ultimately became. The soprano is herself very definitely aware of the development of her acting, and indeed, the deepening of her involvement in her roles. In fact, there are some roles, including that of Puccini's *Suor Angelica,* that Tebaldi has chosen not to sing on stage because she feels their emotional demands would be so tremendous that her singing would be overcome by the inner turmoil of the character.

Tebaldi reflected to me that she might have sung Angelica at the beginning of her career, when she was more reserved on the stage. But, she felt, to have begun singing Angelica after the late 1950s would have drained her too greatly to allow her to give a performance in which music and drama were properly balanced.

It has always been a fascinating pastime to look at the life of an artist and then attempt to relate real-life events to artistic achievement. In Tebaldi's case, one notes that the death of her mother in 1957 probably affected her more than any other event in her entire adult life. The absolute sincerity of Tebaldi's grief at her mother's loss is apparent to all who know her, and it is equally apparent that when Tebaldi returned to the stage in 1958 her ability to express emotion had grown considerably. There is probably a great deal of truth to the axiom that an artist must suffer in order to be receptive to the deepest feelings and to be able to transmit these sentiments through art. People who have closely followed the career of Beverly Sills, for example, swear that after the personal tragedy of giving birth to a severely retarded son and a daughter who is almost totally deaf, Sills returned to her career a more brilliant singer than ever before and a superb actress as well. Even if one does not have to face years of great tragedy in order to achieve greatness as an artist, the correlation between deep suffering and maximum artistic sensitivity is well documented.

Some actors—in both spoken theatre and opera—manage to appear completely different in each new role, adopting a different walk, strikingly varied modes of gesture and facial expressions for every character. In opera, Beverly Sills is one such artist. Other artists, rather than assuming totally new and different characteristics for each role, achieve equally powerful results by finding something within their own personalities that comes uniquely to life in each character. Renata Tebaldi belongs in this category. Tebaldi is not "the same" when she sings Mimi as when she sings Tosca, Maddalena, or Gioconda, but she is recognizably Tebaldi. That is, while there are certain recognizable gestures and facial expressions, as well as means of vocal expression, her characterizations are not interchangeable!

The soprano declares that when she is on stage singing a given role, she feels that she has become the character. It is doubtful that she forgets she is a singer named Renata Tebaldi—despite operatic lore, which abounds in anecdotes concerning singers who claim that they so fully identify with their roles that they all but die when their characters meet their ends. Once some years ago Anna Moffo ended a *Lucia di Lammermoor* "Mad Scene" with a real swoon, and claimed later that she had felt truly transformed into Donizetti's heroine.

However, one assumes that Tebaldi's concentration on her

role is, on most occasions, deep indeed. There is, also a rather thrilling sense of authority which Tebaldi brings to all her work. A given note may go flat or sound strained, but for every role she sings Tebaldi is always totally prepared. I cannot personally recall—nor have I ever heard of—a performance during which she missed a cue or entered an ensemble too early or late. Sheer probability would argue such a memory lapse must have occurred at one time or another, but if so, it cannot have been frequent.

In discussing the histrionic side of opera, Tebaldi is fond of saying that "without personality nothing of any interest can happen on the stage!" How right she is! Tebaldi exudes that indefinable radiance that used to be called "star quality" and more recently has been known as "charisma." However, she is most emphatically not one to cling to the spotlight when the focus of a scene belongs to another artist. A well-known Tebaldi anecdote concerns the time when, after the third act of *Manon Lescaut,* she refused to take a solo bow, saying to the amazed tenor that this act was "his" and therefore only he should have a solo bow! Granted that the roles that she sings are almost invariably the center of attention, Tebaldi seems to command special notice. How she does this is one of the inexplicable aspects of her art . . . one can only say that her bearing, her voice, and her reputation—a Tebaldi appearance is always a special event—all contribute to the aura of magnificence that surrounds her.

The soprano applies a number of her own offstage characteristics to the *persona* that she presents in an opera. Her own love of clothes and interest in fashion insures that whatever Tebaldi wears onstage is flattering, handsome, and worn properly. Her own graciousness is reflected in a myriad of little ways during a performance. The way Tebaldi takes Mario's hands in hers on the lines "No, Mario mio, lascia pria che la preghi, che l'infiori" during the love duet in the first act of *Tosca,* or her delighted smile when the children present Desdemona their flowers in the second act of *Otello,* add so much to her characterizations.

It is also true that in some roles, Tebaldi has shown an inclination to overdo certain moments—sometimes, her pommeling of Scarpia's chest or the excessive force with which she hurled Laura to the ground in *La Gioconda* evoked smiles . . . and yet, these are exactly the ways in which a gentle, kind-natured person might express sudden and impotent rage—through an almost endearingly clumsy method of dealing with the "enemy." It is as if these naive actions may not be the perfect way to handle a stressful situation, but they are *exactly* the way Tebaldi's character would react.

Tebaldi does not subscribe to any one "method" in building a character. Yet her discussion of how she searches for what she considers her character's real reaction to a set of dramatic circumstances cuts to the core of Stanislavsky's approach. Without putting a label to her creative processes, Tebaldi very thoroughly dissects each role and builds her character with the psychological material she finds therein. Therefore, it is not surprising that Tebaldi, who is tall and, in her words, "*robusta*" of figure, manages to appear slight and frail as Mimi. Her shy gait, her modest smile and seeming weakness is very real—and very different from the self-assured figure she cuts as Floria Tosca!

Without denigrating the importance of the visual side of Tebaldi's artistry, it must be concluded that she will be best remembered in the history of opera for her vocal achievements. The lustre of tone that was hers throughout her peak years of singing has seldom been equalled. The warmth of sound, the simple elegance of phrasing, and the artistic honesty that Tebaldi has lavished on every role in her repertoire is virtually unparalleled among singers.

Although Renata Tebaldi professes that she will never teach singing, the recordings she has made will serve as models for future generations of sopranos. Already, one hears young artists in major opera houses who have obviously listened closely to Tebaldi's recordings and live performances. In fact, Tebaldi's art speaks most clearly through this legacy of sterling performances, which will undoubtedly be a source of inspiration for years to come!

Tebaldi as Madama Butterfly
at the Metropolitan in 1958 (Melançon).

The Recordings

Renata Tebaldi could hardly have been active at a more favorable era for recordings. Hitting her early prime at the beginning of the age of the long-playing record, and remaining in peak form through the development of stereophonic sound, the soprano has created a living library of performances of virtually all her stage roles, her concert pieces, and a number of roles that she never sang onstage: Santuzza, the three heroines of *Il Trittico,* Liu in *Turandot,* Amelia in *Un Ballo in Maschera,* and the *Trovatore* Leonora. "Pirated" discs available to the collector who knows where to look offer the soprano as *Fedora, Giovanna d'Arco,* Helen of Troy (in *Mefistofele*) and others; while dozens of privately recorded tapes of actual performances document many of the finest evenings in her career, and feature Tebaldi singing with artists with whom she never made commercial recordings.

In this chapter each of Renata Tebaldi's commercial recordings will be discussed, as will a selection of the more important and most generally available of the "pirated" recordings. (Please note that recital discs which are comprised of cuts taken from the soprano's recordings of complete operas, as opposed to those which were specially recorded, have not been discussed at length but are listed in the discography.)

COMPLETE OPERAS

BOITO: *MEFISTOFELE*

One wonders, in retrospect, how Sir Rudolf Bing managed to neglect *Mefistofele* throughout his twenty-two-year tenure at the Metropolitan. Having the services of Cesare Siepi, Tebaldi, and Del Monaco (the principal artists on the London recording), not to mention those of Carlo Bergonzi, Antonietta Stella, Gabriella Tucci, Bonaldo Giaiotti, Nicolai Ghiaurov, and several others at his disposal, Bing could have given us many "Golden Age" calibre performances of this complex opera. It took Julius Rudel, making do with a roster of City Opera artists who—with the very important exceptions of Norman Treigle and Gilda Cruz-Romo—could not begin to do justice to Boito's music, to make *Mefistofele* a success with New York audiences. This visually stunning production was created for Treigle, and was occasionally graced by Cruz-Romo as Marguerita and Elena in 1969.

Before that production, one had to be content in the United States with the London recording, while one New York audience was treated to a concert performance of the opera by the American Opera Society in 1968. This performance, starring Ghiaurov, Tebaldi, and Bergonzi, with Lamberto Gardelli conducting, has been preserved in a pirated album and will be discussed as such later.

The London recording, therefore, provided many people with their only exposure to this work for many years. With the Orchestra and Chorus of L'Accademia di Santa Cecilia led by Serafin, this set featured London-Decca's favorite Italian soprano, bass, and tenor of the time. In a recent revelation, it became generally known that Giuseppe di Stefano had originally been engaged for the role of Faust, but withdrew after recording about two-thirds of his role and was replaced by Del Monaco. Much of the fruits of these early sessions were released by London-Decca in the spring of 1973, providing the only nonpirated recording featuring Tebaldi and di Stefano together. More about this one below . . .

Tebaldi appears on this recording only as Margherita, leaving the role of her operatic debut, Helen of Troy, to a decidedly less accomplished artist, Florinda Cavalli. Both of Margherita's scenes go well for the soprano, who seems conventionally naive in the Garden Scene, although her sweetness of tone will, for many, make up for a lack of deep characterization here. Tebaldi hits full stride in the prison scene, singing "L'altra notte in fondo al mare" with electrifying conviction and a haunting projection of the words. In "Lontano, lontano, lontano," Tebaldi and Del Monaco blend their voices together all but perfectly, and the soprano's lyricism in Margherita's death scene is spellbinding. Her final "Enrico, mi fai ribrezzo" is a knockout!

In general, Del Monaco's Faust disappoints; he often is strident and forces his way through the score. Siepi is elegant and imposing, lacking a little of the beastly fury that Ghiaurov and Treigle have been known to impart to the role. Serafin's firm and knowledgable conducting and the fine work of the chorus in the prologue make for an otherwise excellent performance.

Turning to the "appendix" to the complete *Mefistofele* released in 1973, Tebaldi in the Garden Scene is, once again, fresh of voice and just a bit cool. "L'altra notte" is, in this earlier "take," somewhat less dramatically dynamic than on the one released on the complete set. Her Margherita is more withdrawn, commenting sadly upon her situation, but not fully realizing the terror that faces her. In the final moments Tebaldi once more creates a vivid study of the dying, demented girl. Di Stefano, more basically well suited to the role of Faust than Del Monaco, sings in ravishing fashion, except for some disconcertingly flat high notes, which may or may not have provided him with reason for withdrawing. If these excerpts shed little new light on the opera, the Margherita of Tebaldi, or the Fiend of Siepi (who sounds even more elegant and "clean-cut" here than on the complete set), they are still valid for collectors for the pairing of di Stefano and Tebaldi for the only time on discs.

BOITO: *MEFISTOFELE* (Pirated Recording)

This pirated set, made from tapes of a 1968 Carnegie Hall performance by the American Opera Society, surrounds Tebaldi with such estimable artists as Nicolai Ghiaurov in the title role and Carlo Bergonzi as Faust, with Lamberto Gardelli conducting. In this performance, Tebaldi sang both Margherita and Elena. If her singing of Margherita is fresher and more youthful on the Decca-London set, Tebaldi projects Margherita's madness and suffering even more vividly in the live performance, "L'altra notte" is given a particularly electrifying reading here. In this instance the soprano blends text and music perfectly, finding the essence of the Italian lyric drama in this piece. Joined by Bergonzi, Tebaldi offers a haunting account of "Lontano, lontano, lontano" and goes on to "die" with tremendous effect.

Tebaldi's Elena finds her in good form, singing with abandon and faithfulness to the line. Since Rudolph Bing's Metropolitan Opera could have cast *Mefistofele* so well throughout his entire tenure there, this performance by three of the Met's finest singers only points up what New Yorkers were deprived of! Bergonzi's lyrical, tastefully vocalized Faust and Ghiaurov's fearsomely acted and magnificently sung Devil make up what must certainly be the finest account of this music in New York for decades. It should be noted in passing that Julius Rudel's New York City Opera production of *Mefistofele* was more memorable for its stunning production than for the level of singing, except on nights when Treigle's Mefisto was partnered by Gilda Cruz-Romo as Margherita and Elena. No City Opera tenor singing Faust came anywhere near to approaching Bergonzi. The sixth side of the three-disc MRF set (MRF 4) is comprised of scenes from other U.S. performances of the opera. These include a Chicago performance of "Lontano, lontano, lontano" attractively sung by Tebaldi and Alfredo Kraus.

CATALANI: *LA WALLY*

Having recorded virtually her entire repertoire, in many cases twice, it was not surprising that Tebaldi and London-Decca ventured into unfamiliar territory with their 1968 recording of Catalani's *La Wally* an opera that was a great favorite of Toscanini's—and, in truth, of practically no one else! Tebaldi had sung the role in the 1950s at La Scala (with Renata Scotto wearing Gualtiero's trousers!) but not in the States, or any other major Italian theatre. Whatever the limitations of the libretto (a rather unappetizing saga of a girl who can't seem to make her mind up about the tenor, whom at various points she strikes, has thrown over a cliff, and commits suicide for) the score offers some interesting touches, some lovely arias for soprano, and a reasonably stirring final duet, climaxed by an avalanche that finally does the unfortunate tenor, Giuseppe Haggensbach, in.

The role doesn't lie very high for soprano, and if in 1968 Tebaldi's basic sound was somewhat harder in quality than previously, her stunning deployment of her chest tones and unflinching handling of the most demanding passages make for an engrossing and moving performance. If the top notes in "Ebbene, ne andrò lontano" are somewhat stressful, in Tebaldi's singing the aria has a contemplative, wistful quality that is entirely appropriate. Wally's third act aria, is sung with special richness of tone, and, indeed, only in the fourth act music directly before Hagenbach's entrance does Tebaldi seem dangerously tired. The duet that closes the opera, though, finds her in full control once more, and the strength with which she delivers the anguished, spoken cries of "Giuseppe" after the avalanche (as well as the second act curtain line, "Io lo vo morto" after the tenor has insulted her by soliciting a kiss at a town dance) is quite fantastic!

Tebaldi's colleagues here include Mario Del Monaco as Giuseppe. His voice, while still powerful, is quite colorless and ineffective except when he sings fortissimo, which, in this recording, is too often anyway. Also in the cast are Piero Cappuccilli as Gelner, the tenor's rival and occasional nemesis, who sings with menace and a dark, attractive sound, Justino Diaz as Wally's father, and Lydia Malimpietri as Gualtiero, a *travesti* role. The Monte Carlo Opera Chorus and Orchestra are vigorously and sympathetically conducted by Fausto Cleva.

CATALANI: *LA WALLY* (Pirated Recording)

The American Opera Society's 1968 concert performance of Catalani's most popular (!) opera has been pressed onto a pirated set that will please the soprano's and the composer's admirers. March of '68 found Tebaldi in her post-Gioconda "dramatic" period. The voice is darker in color than in earlier times, and high notes are apt to be metallic, but there is a genuine authority to her singing and a stylish command of Catalani's musical vocabulary. Compared to her complete London-Decca performance of the title role, which was recorded only four months after the Carnegie Hall event, the soprano's voice sounds marginally richer in the resonant Carnegie Hall acoustics. Wally's two major arias are compellingly vocalized, with "Ebbene, ne andrò lontano" far superior in this version to the "commercial" release, where there is a certain tentativeness in Tebaldi's singing. Another plus to this recording is the warm and colorful singing by Carlo Bergonzi in the role of Hagenbach. Bergonzi's warm and lyrical approach to the role is far more successful than that of Del Monaco, who was, in 1968, unable to sing softly with ease or effect. Lamberto Gardelli is a most sympathetic and supportive conductor.

CILEA: *ADRIANA LECOUVREUR*

Tebaldi recorded her "pet project" in 1961, in anticipation of the Metropolitan revival that followed a year behind schedule, in 1963. The set is extravagantly cast, with Del Monaco as Maurizio and Simionato as the Princess de Bouillon.

The soprano performs her favorite role with interpretative vigor, musical finesse, and glowing sound. Tebaldi's voice was at its fullest, grandest estate when this set was made, and the volume of sound she could produce in the duets with Del Monaco and Simionato is staggering. Of course, she phrases with customary delicacy in her two arias, and declaims the *Phèdre* excerpt with lavalike intensity. Adriana's death scene is sung with power and, importantly, excellent taste, while the confrontation with the Princess at the close of Act Two is a knockout.

Del Monaco and Simionato each offer distinguished, indeed, definitive accounts of their music, while the role of Michonnet is more than capably sung by Giulio Fioravanti. Franco Capuana conducts with elegant crispness.

GIORDANO: *ANDREA CHENIER*

The Everest-Cetra budget release of the Giordano opera stems from an RAI concert performance of the early 1950s. Tebaldi's exceedingly fresh singing of Maddalena is the strongest point of the album. As in the later London set, Tebaldi captures the drama of the part, and delivers a stunning "La mama morta," while the duets with the tenor are notable for the richness of her tone. Unfortunately, the supporting cast, including José Soler as Chenier and Ugo Savarese as Gerard, are of minimal interest. Arturo Basile is the conductor.

GIORDANO: *ANDREA CHENIER*

London's *Chenier* set was one of its first stereophonic opera recordings, released in 1958. Here, Tebaldi is matched with artists who can meet her on her own vocal terms. In general, the soprano sounds hardly less youthful than on the Cetra recording, singing with utmost clarity of sound and total accuracy of pitch. Furthermore, the two great duets between Maddalena and Chenier are properly balanced here, as Mario Del Monaco offers a fervent and vocally strong account of the title role. Completing the trio of stellar assignments in this performance is Ettore Bastianini as Gerard, a role that takes off with his darkly handsome voice and dramatic thrust. His third act scene with the soprano is vastly superior to that provided by Savarese on the Cetra performance. Completing the cast are such fine artists as Piero de Palma as the spy, and, in a very early assignment, Fiorenza Cossotto as the heroine's maid, La Bersi. The Orchestra and Chorus of L'Accademia di Santa Cecilia are crisply led by Gianandrea Gavazzeni.

Turning now to Tebaldi's contribution, her sympathy to both the character of Maddalena and the music is most apparent. Maddalena belongs to a rather conventional breed of operatic heroines, not terribly bright, rather helpless, but "good" and loyal, ultimately sacrificing life itself in order to be united in death with her lover . . . and, of course, ready to bargain away her "honor" if its loss can save her lover's life. One thinks, of course, of Tosca (an even more passionate and stronger fighter than the gentle Maddalena), the *Trovatore* Leonora, and Minnie in *La Fanciulla del West* (who wins, for once) as Maddalena's nearest cousins.

Dramatically, the role consists of a series of sudden mood changes on Maddalena's part. Arch at the beginning of Act One, she is arch; in Act Two, which takes place some five years later, she is first desolate and frightened, then lifted to ecstasy in the duet with the tenor, and finally more plunged into despair at the end of the act. The third act finds Maddalena at her most resolute, and in her offer to sacrifice her "honor" for Chenier, at her most attractive. Act Four has the girl heroically going to her death with Chenier, saving the doomed woman Legray in the process, and meeting her end with great, if rather incongruous glee. (Certainly the curtain line "Viva la morte insieme" is one of the most nonsensical endings in all opera—the words actually mean "Long live death together!") This heroine, then, is neither terribly well drawn or brilliantly motivated dramatically speaking. Yet Tebaldi cloaks Maddalena with her own surpassing femininity, making her gentle yet strong, providing a sense of humanity for a character who in the bare reading of the libretto appears stiff and hard to bring to life. Of course, Giordano has given Maddalena some pretty exciting and often very expressive music to sing, but Tebaldi's adroit phrasing propels the music still further, making it sound truly great.

One of Tebaldi's unique gifts is her ability to make so much of individual words or phrases . . . in the second act duet, for example, listen to the chilling terror implicit in the words "Ho paura" as she searches for the poet Chenier; in the same scene, moments later, her phrasing of the words "Erivate possente" suggests so well the heroine's sense of powerlessness. Of course, in the third act, Tebaldi's bitter and crushed cry of "Prendimi" to Gerard as she begins "La mamma morta" is the quintessence of *verismo* style. The anguished shriek uttered by the soprano as Chenier is sentenced to death at the end of Act Three is rather jarring, but, since it has occurred in every Tebaldi Maddalena that I recall hearing, is evidently an effect dearly loved by the soprano. Although this moment is anything but subtle, it certainly fits well into the rough and tumble—and almost always effective—Giordano score. Tebaldi's performance, of course, is made up of far more than a series of outstanding moments. Her voice has seldom been more perfectly controlled than here. The soprano lightens her tone for such delicate sections as Maddalena's narration of her current troubles to Chenier at the beginning of the second act love duet, and then broadens her attack, giving vent to full projection of the final portion of that duet, "Ora soave." "La mamma morta" is sensitively performed, with Tebaldi sounding no more overwrought in the music than is absolutely necessary. Indeed, the rather bloodcurdling text is projected in hushed tones, underscoring through understatement the numbing experiences described by Maddalena. The chest register is handsomely deployed, sounding opulent and never overdone, while the upper register is clear and free, enabling Tebaldi to soar up to the optional higher ending of the aria.

No *Chenier* performance can succeed unless that mad and glorious final duet is well sung, and this recording does not let down here either. Singing with an abandon that is positively infectious, Tebaldi and Del Monaco convince the listener that there is no happier fate possible for two lovers than their union in death! The fact that in the final two lines of the duet Tebaldi's tone takes on a slightly harder than usual (in 1958) edge matters not in the least, given the power and conviction of her singing. *Andrea Chenier* is an opera loved best by devotees of Italian-style singing and scorned by those with less sympathy for this noncerebral type of opera. *Chenier* may be anything but deep, but given a high quality reading such as this, it is a highly effective and memorable operatic experience.

GIORDANO: *FEDORA* (Pirated Recording)

This pirated recording offers a San Carlo performance, circa 1961, of the Giordano showpiece, which Tebaldi sang in Chicago as well as Italy. Conducted by Arturo Basile, the performance costarred Giuseppe di Stefano as Loris and Mario Sereni as Di Siriex.

Judging from this recording, Tebaldi was an exciting Fedora, although in the first act, there is a sense of heaviness and fatigue in her voice that foreshadows the problems of 1963. In the opening moments, and, in truth, for a few measures in the second act, there are some pitch problems as well. To her credit, there is fire and authority to Tebaldi's work, making the vengeful Russian princess a vivid figure, and her voice often rings out with its accustomed beauty, as in Fedora's oath of vengeance at the end of the first act. The long duet with Loris in Act Two is quite good, its opening, *parlando* section being exceptionally well done, while the passionate final portion is excitingly performed (although Tebaldi eschews the optional high C).

Act Three is Tebaldi's best work of the evening, with her voice sounding freer and more velvety than in the first two acts. Tebaldi's handling of the death scene represents *verismo* acting of the first order, with an unforgettable cry of "Loris, dove sei?" Di Stefano is an ardent Loris, singing "Amor ti vieta" handsomely with little sign of strain. Sereni is more than adequate as the French diplomat Di Siriex. Admirers of Tebaldi and the entire *Fedora* cult will enjoy this set, which is, incidentally, rather well engineered.

MASCAGNI: *CAVALLERIA RUSTICANA*

With the 1974 rerelease on London-Decca of this set, originally mastered by RCA in 1958, but missing from record shops since 1965, a beautiful performance will once again provide a thrilling listening experience.

Recorded in Florence with the Orchestra and Chorus of the Maggio Musicale Fiorentino, we have Tebaldi in still another role that she has yet to sing on stage. This is a pity, for she is so well suited to the role vocally. Captured in 1958, Tebaldi's studio Santuzza is sung with throbbingly rich, ample tone, with special emphasis on the low notes and chest tones, although these are never overdone. While the placid, rather uninteresting conducting by Alberto Erede is not geared to the fierce drama of Mascagni's opera, Tebaldi finds means of expressing Santuzza's torment. Her "Voi lo sapete, o mamma" is awesome . . . listen to those accents on "L'amai, l'amai, l'amai!"! Joined by Jussi Bjoerling, in superb form in his second recorded Turiddu, Tebaldi makes the confrontation with Turiddu the major scene in the opera, as indeed it should be . . . how pregnant with fury is her cursing of Turiddu at the duet's conclusion.

Listening to this recording in 1974 gives the lie to the claim that Tebaldi never acted her roles before the mid-1960s. Her Santuzza is a warm-blooded, rather sympathetic creature, whose deep hurt forces her to erupt with deadly hatred. And yet Tebaldi makes the listener believe in her remorse in the duet with Alfio, so brightly and forcefully performed by Ettore Bastianini.

It is strange that this recording, highly revered by many, through some quirk in marketing never became a cornerstone of the RCA catalogue (indeed, it was prematurely withdrawn). Hopefully, in its new incarnation on London-Decca, it will do better.

PONCHIELLI: *LA GIOCONDA*

Recorded directly after the first of Tebaldi's two Metropolitan seasons in the title role of Ponchielli's opera, the London-Decca *La Gioconda* captures one of Tebaldi's finest portrayals with clarity and accuracy. Along with Minnie in *La Fanciulla del West*, a not dissimilar role, Gioconda was certainly one of

Tebaldi's two greatest achievements in the post-1963 period, and her stage performances are well documented by this studio production.

To dwell on Gioconda's many vocal challenges for the singer is to state the obvious. The role alternates lyrical and very dramatic singing all too frequently to be kind to the human voice. Furthermore, Gioconda operates on quite a high level of emotion most of the time.

Any comparison of this 1967 recording to earlier Tebaldi discs is foolish, for Gioconda is quite different from the roles she generally sang fifteen years earlier. On its own terms, her work is remarkable here. The basic sound is full and rounded, with a sense of power and confidence as well. The many high Cs are strong and secure, although their production is more than a little effortful. It goes without saying that there is more to any role than disconnected high notes, and Tebaldi's handling of Gioconda's sweeping phrases, as in "O cor, dono funesto," the entire scene with Laura in Act Two, and in the killingly demanding fourth act, place Tebaldi's Gioconda in her great tradition! Vocally secure throughout virtually her entire range, Tebaldi offers a Gioconda of splendid vocal and dramatic contrasts. Her mastery of the quiet phrase, as when echoing La Cieca's "A te questo rosario" to Laura in the fourth act, has rarely been more apparent, while the musical brilliance of the aria "Suicidio" (also recorded on the 1964 recital disc ranks with the finest versions that one can find on disc or in the opera house. Dramatically, the character is almost a patchwork, now the devoted daughter, now vicious, a scorned mistress, eventually heroically self-destructive—and thus difficult to act coherently, let alone convincingly.

The key to Renata Tebaldi's Gioconda is femininity. She allows the tormented street-singer a basic personality of rather appealing warmth, which, of course, ignites when roused by the various complications of the libretto. Therefore, Tebaldi finds ample opportunity to spin a soft line, as in Act One when she leaves her mother to search for Enzo, or later in that act when she pleads with Alvise to spare poor La Cieca from the mob, or in her unearthly "Son la Gioconda" as she reveals her identity to Laura in Act Two. Tebaldi has no fear of the most wracking moments, finding ample volume and power for "L'amo come il fulgor" and the strenuous finale to Act Two, as well as the rather hilarious line "O madre mia, quanto mi costi" in Act Three. In the fourth act, Tebaldi's intensity never flags, creating as close an illusion of a theatrical performance as one will find on any operatic disc.

Gioconda, as is well known, has six choice roles for singers, and even the artist in the title part—the choicest role, to be sure—must interact musically and dramatically with her colleagues. As it happens, the support is better musically than dramatically, as no one is prepared in this performance to offer the hot-blooded excitement that surges through Tebaldi's work.

Marilyn Horne, not usually associated with late nineteenth century Italian opera, offers an aristocratic, smoothly sung Laura, devoid of Horne's usual chestiness, and lacking a degree of passion. Her part in "L'amo come il fulgor del creato" is dignified and supple, but hardly a histrionic match for Tebaldi (find a tape of the 1968 Met broadcast of *Gioconda* and listen to Tebaldi and Cossotto perform this music!). As Enzo, Carlo Bergonzi sings generously, which is about all one must ask of anyone performing this shallow role. Robert Merrill also sings attractively as Barnaba, but offers nothing at all in the way of characterization, which in this role is a crime! Merrill doesn't even bother to scream in rage as the curtain falls upon Gioconda's suicide—he simply "walks through" the entire opera. Oralia Dominguez is attractive and musical as poor old Cieca, while Nicolai Ghiuselev is a somewhat lightweight Alvise Badoero. Lamberto Gardelli's bright, extroverted reading of the score is a tremendous help, and the entire performance is colorful and pleasant to hear. Ideally, the full cast would have matched Tebaldi's commitment to the score, but the net effect of this recording is immensely satisfactory!

PUCCINI: *LA BOHÈME*

Tebaldi's first complete opera recordings were *La Bohème, Tosca, Madama Butterfly, Otello* and *Aïda,* made between the years 1950 and 1952. *La Bohème* pairs the soprano with Giancinto

Prandelli as Rodolfo, with a cast that also included Hilde Gueden as Musetta, Giovanni Inghilleri as Marcello, Fernando Corena as Schaunard, and Alberto Erede conducting the Orchestra and Chorus of L'Accademia di Santa Cecilia, Rome. Except for Gueden, a musically and histrionically refined grisette, and the novelty of Corena in a baritone role, the supporting cast is not distinguished. Tebaldi, however, already an experienced Mimi, reveals an extraordinary affinity for this character, singing with a direct sincerity and a simplicity that is quite irresistible. The finest singing here is found in the third act, where Tebaldi succeeds in recreating Mimi's anguish over her failing health and her difficulties with Rodolfo, singing with endless warmth and ample volume of sound. If Tebaldi always tended to emphasize Mimi's sadness—as stressing the heroine's lighthearted moments—she did not overdraw the portrait into unrelieved sentimentality. The duets with Prandelli are in the main successful, although the tenor's voice was too light to be a perfect mate to Tebaldi's fuller tones. Prandelli was, though, a sensitive singer, and his Rodolfo is gentle and appealing if not first class. Erede's conducting is generally sympathetic although often routine, rising to the excitement of "O soave fanciulla" and, for example, the second act finale, but being somewhat lethargic elsewhere.

PUCCINI: *LA BOHÈME*

The inevitable stereophonic remake of *Bohème* offers a performance of unique vocal gloss. In addition to Tebaldi's Mimi, Carlo Bergonzi's Rodolfo, Ettore Bastianini's Marcello, Cesare Siepi's Colline, the two comic turns by Fernando Corena, and Tullio Serafin's conducting are all of high level. Only the shrill and often below-pitch Musetta of Gianna D'Angelo is a serious drawback.

Tebaldi sings Mimi with what had become for her "predictable" warmth. By this time (1959) she had grown to see Mimi as an adult, gentle soul, able to give herself fully in love; thus ingenuousness is not a key characteristic of her Mimi. What the soprano brings to the character is a richness of sound and a secureness of pitch, and a touching, if somewhat knowing, approach to Mimi's personality. This lack of completely youthful abandon is also traceable to Serafin's tempi, which make the performance appealing to Puccini's more sentimental devotees. Serafin, viewing the work as an expression of bittersweet emotion rather than an enthusiastic portrayal of the world of the young, lingers on all the most poignant moments, filtering the score through a haze of nostalgic remembrances. The result is a slowly paced reading that presents some awesome vocal moments. Thus, Tebaldi is encouraged to spin out phrase after phrase of lyrical, gossamer tone (as in "Mi chiamono Mimi"), and is allowed, ultimately, to expire gently. In between, her work is vocally pristine (although the high C with Bergonzi at the end of Act One is a little labored by both artists), and the entire Third Act is especially rewarding for the listener. Somehow, though, Tebaldi's earlier Mimi is a fresher, more striking conception. This second *Bohēme* is sung by a great artist at the height of her powers, but is less vividly colored than the younger Tebaldi's effort.

Bergonzi's Rodolfo ranks with the best, which is to say Jussi Bjoerling on the Beecham recording, and Beniamino Gigli on the ancient Rome Opera performance, reissued of late by Seraphim. Bastianini lavishes his superior artistry upon Marcello, who has never seemed a more appealing and interesting character than here, while Siepi sings Colline with characteristic vocal integrity, making much, as might be expected, of the "cloak" aria.

PUCCINI: *LA FANCIULLA DEL WEST*

London-Decca's 1958 recording of Puccini's "oater" must have seemed risky at the time, in that it predated the Metropolitan's immensely successful revivals of the 1960s with Leontyne Price and Dorothy Kirsten, and of course, the 1970 edition with Tebaldi as Minnie.

Fortunately, this recording succeeds musically, and it might justifiably receive a good deal of credit for popularizing the opera in this country in the past fifteen years.

Minnie, a sort of Wild West Tosca who doesn't have to resort to violence (she only cheats at poker) to wrest the suffering tenor from the nasty baritone (Jack Rance is not nearly as wicked as Scarpia), is incongruous to Americans and Englishmen familiar with U.S. western law—imagine reading the Bible in a saloon! Some purists even find the poker-cheating episode distasteful, as this makes Minnie clearly no Girl Scout of the Golden West. Still, on her own terms, Minnie is a delightful character (and one of two Puccini heroines who is alive and happily in love at the final curtain) and Tebaldi brings her to life most charmingly in this recording.

To begin with, her voice is opulent and free from strain, with high Cs on pitch if tinged with metal. The middle register is as meltingly warm as ever, and Tebaldi brings an intuitive sense of romance and Minnie's own innocence to the role. Wisely, she plays the character straight, cheerfully unconcerned with the anachronisms and little absurdities that make Minnie a trifle arch and difficult to accept for those who spent every Saturday afternoon of their childhoods watching westerns at the local movie palace. Surmounting the pistol-packin' Act One entrance, and even passing out cigars with a charming Spanish inflection (this Minnie could even get a job as a cigarette girl at the Copacabana!), Tebaldi discovers a veritable gold mine of tone in the "Laggiù nel Soledad" monologue, making its climactic phrase "S'amavan tanto . . ." as worthy a prize as all the ore south of San Francisco.

Reining in her voice to suggest a youthful, vulnerable Minnie, the soprano almost convinces us that she has never been kissed before the first act curtain.

Of course, in Act Two, Minnie demonstrates that she is a full-fledged Puccini heroine, and here Tebaldi is properly forceful and agitated. The poker game scene, played quite honestly, without undue affectation, is marvelously tense, capped as it is by Tebaldi's chesty cry of "Tre asci e un paio" as she wins the game with a hand dealt from her garter belt.

In Act Three, the soprano handles Minnie's high-flying offstage cries with ease, and then lavishes every sweet note at her command on the cowboys who would lynch Dick Johnson

—and the listeners who, like the onstage assemblage, will ultimately be able to deny her nothing.

Tebaldi is ably supported here by Del Monaco's straightforward and athletically appealing Dick Johnson. The tenor's voice is notably clear and easily projected, particularly in the second act aria "Or son sei mesi" and the showpiece "Ch'ella mi creda libero e lontano" in Act Three.

Cornell MacNeil offers a rock-solid and idiomatic Rance, while Giorgio Tozzi milks the blind storyteller's song for everything it's worth. Franco Capuana leads the Santa Cecilia forces with spirit, and Decca's engineers create an authentic snowstorm for Act Two . . . in short, a jolly and endearing performance all around.

PUCCINI: *MADAMA BUTTERFLY*

This first Tebaldi recording of *Butterfly* is one of the soprano's very best achievements in the recording studio, for here all the youthful radiance of her voice is matched by mature power and a full-bodied characterization that acutely realizes the unique combination of child and woman that is Cio-cio-san. Eschewing the high D flat in Butterfly's entrance Tebaldi sings with tonal security, an abundance of gorgeous, freely flowing sound, and high notes that, although they often take on a slightly metallic but exciting edge, are on pitch and easily produced.

PUCCINI: *MADAMA BUTTERFLY*

By the late 1950s, with stereophonic sound firmly established, London-Decca felt obliged to rerecord a number of the operas produced in monaural sound in the early part of the decade. Thus, new stereo issues of these operas were made and the mono sets relegated to the budget labels, where they remain to this day. Renata Tebaldi was invited to head the cast of the remakes of all the operas she had first done in mono, with the exception of *La Traviata*, which was assigned to Joan Sutherland.

Madama Butterfly, the first of these remakes, was recorded in 1958, by which time the soprano had added the role to her onstage credits. She first performed it in the opera house at Barcelona, marking her return to the stage after nearly six months absence after the death of her mother. Vocally, 1958 was an especially good year for Tebaldi. The "crisis" of 1963 was five years off; Tebaldi, then in her mid-thirties, had the utmost vocal power at her command, with little noticeable loss of freshness of sound. This time, in recording *Madama Butterfly,* London-Decca surrounded Tebaldi with some of the finest talent then available: tenor Carlo Bergonzi, appearing for the first time on records with Tebaldi; the revered Maestro Tullio Serafin conducting, and, as Suzuki, Fiorenza Cossotto, at that time on the verge of her international renown.

This performance, amiably and knowingly directed by Serafin, who did have a tendency to linger over the more tender moments, emphasizes vocal "gold." Tebaldi, for all her identification with the character, sounds even less like a fifteen-year-old than on the earlier edition, so the drama appears to center on the problems of a fully grown Italian (as opposed to Japanese) lady . . . yet seldom did she sound more honey-toned than here. Once past Butterfly's entrance, in which she does really sound too matronly, Tebaldi offers a passionate and "sincere" interpretation, suggesting frailty and vulnerability, if not adolescence. All of Cio-cio-san's most poignant moments are lovingly presented. "Io seguo il mio destino" and "Vogliatemi bene" in Act One, the letter duet in Act Two, Butterfly's surrender of the child in Act Three ("Sopra il bel velo del cielo") are tender and charming. Furthermore, Tebaldi has ample power to ride over the orchestra in the "big" moments of the love duet, "Un bel dì" and the final scene. Tebaldi's Butterfly, a natural resident of the Italian opera house rather than a modest home in Nagasaki, is a close-to-perfect fusion of the exotic aura that Puccini worked toward in his score and the Italian idiom that must dominate the opera.

Carlo Bergonzi, surely the possessor of the most beautiful tenor voice of the 1960s, offers an ardent account of Pinkerton. Bergonzi, who, to be sure, makes little attempt to characterize the lieutenant as anything other than a standard Italian tenor, sings with easy eloquence, and his rich, pleasing tone blends happily with Tebaldi's in the love duet. Cossotto is a predictably strong Suzuki, providing excellent support throughout, and singing brilliantly in the flower duet. She is quite likely the finest and most gifted Suzuki to be found on records. Completing the quartet of principles is Enzo Sordello, whose Sharpless is acceptable but plagued by a heavy vibrato. Other recordings of *Madama Butterfly* offer beautiful singing, and the vintage EMI set presents the heartrending and electrifying (if very shrilly sung) Cio-cio-san of Toti Dal Monte, but this recording must be considered the most lavishly cast and opulently sung version of the score on disc.

PUCCINI: *MANON LESCAUT*

This recording, also one of London-Decca's first attempts at stereophonic recording, is somewhat lopsidedly cast (Del Monaco was not an ideal choice for Des Grieux, and Mario Borriello is undistinguished as Lescaut) but allows Tebaldi to show off in one of her finest roles.

Manon, of course is supposed to be a very young girl—a teen-ager, in fact. Massenet, composing his *Manon* for a lyric coloratura, worked with a lighter tonal palette than did Puccini, whose Manon Lescaut is called upon to sing much full-blown, passionate music. The role almost always necessitates use of a *lirico spinto* soprano, whose bigger, heavier sound suggests more maturity than would be ideal for the character. This incongruity of character and music is most apparent in the first act, when Manon, still quite possibly a virgin, meets and runs away with Des Grieux. Thus it is here that Tebaldi's voice sounds just a trifle heavy for Manon Lescaut, nor does she give a line such as "Vedete, io son fedele alla parola mia" its full due of girlishness. This reservation aside, it can be said that Tebaldi provides full measure of all the grown-up passion with which Puccini endowed his sixteen-year-old heroine. Manon may be young chronologically, but she grows up quite rapidly, first in the arms of Des Grieux and later in Geronte's. There is nothing false about Tebaldi's conception of the character after the first act. Tebaldi's womanly feeling makes the second scene with Des Grieux into the musical and dramatic high point of the entire opera. Her mixture of self reproach is precisely what is called for by the composer, and, indeed, the Abbē Prēvost. Vocally, Tebaldi is in prime form. All of her fabled amplitude of sound is present here, and there is ease of production throughout her range, with climactic high notes sounding slightly steely but reached without obvious effort. Tebaldi's *piano* singing is exemplary, with the "In quelle trine morbide" showing off the soprano's fullest dynamic range. In the third act ensemble that precedes the tenor's pleas to be allowed to accompany Manon to Louisiana, Tebaldi sings with remarkable limpidity of sound, remaining distinctly audible without forcing. The fourth act is sung with commitment, with the "Sola, perduta, abbandonata" coming off with special fire and a sense of the heroine's utter exhaustion.

Indeed, Tebaldi's sensitivity to Puccini's dynamic markings of the score serves to underline Del Monaco's tonal rigidity. His tendency to bellow his music is all too apparent here, giving the impression that the Chavalier Des Grieux is in a constant state of hysteria, which is to exaggerate this admittedly unhappy character beyond all reason. Listening to the two singers in the final scene generates a great deal of resistance to Del Monaco, whereas Tebaldi suggests heartbreak and the death of hope without resorting to excesses.

Crisply conducted by Francesco Molinari-Pradelli, the recording boasts Fernando Corena as Geronte, a role which offers this artist the opportunity for a change to portray a vicious man instead of a jolly one. If it can be said with some justice that Puccini's *Manon* is topheavy in the composer's concern for the two lovers over all the other characters (not the case with Massenet's work), it is equally true that on this recording Tebaldi narrows this concern even further, given Del Monaco's less than satisfactory performance.

PUCCINI: *TOSCA*

In this first recording, *Tosca* leaves a number of qualities to be desired. Made before Decca-London opted for "all-star" recordings, much of the blame for the performance's lack of total effect may be attributed to Erede's slack conducting and a Baron Scarpia sung in less than full-blooded, menacing fashion by Enzo Mascherini. Tebaldi's Tosca, however, had yet to fully develop, and this early incarnation is less vividly or commandingly portrayed than one has grown to expect. Moreover, she is in less than perfect vocal form here, with a number of the high Cs being forced and pinched. Still, in the lyrical moments, Tebaldi's charm as an actress and her skill as a singer are as rewarding as ever. "Non la sospiri" in Act One and much of the love duet in Act Three are consummately performed, with Tebaldi handsomely partnered by the Mario Cavarodossi of Giuseppe Campora. The crucial second act scene with Scarpia is, as previously noted, less than completely electrifying, but "Vissi d'arte" is sung with emotion and poise, and the first act encounter between the diva and the Baron is notable for the depth of Tosca's despair over her supposed betrayal by Mario.

In addition to Campora's attractive and idiomatic Cavarodossi, the recording features Fernando Corena's first of several recorded Sacrestans and the succinctly understated and very effective Spoletta of Piero de Palma. Those who own neither of Tebaldi's recordings of this opera would be best advised to select the later performance (to be discussed below), but this first of Tebaldi's *Tosca*s currently available in a budget edition on Richmond, offers a number of rewards to the soprano's devotees.

PUCCINI: *TOSCA*

The first London-Decca *Tosca* was the weakest of Tebaldi's first complete opera recordings; in terms of totality of effect, the stereo version of 1958 is a distinct if not complete improvement. The producers wisely reengaged the three most effective members of the earlier cast—Tebaldi, Corena (as the Sacrestan), and Piero de Palma (as Spoletta)—and added Mario Del Monaco and George London as Mario and Scarpia, while engaging Francesco Molinari-Pradelli to conduct, once again, the Orchestra and Chorus of L'Accademia di Santa Cecilia.

Tebaldi's conception of the heroine had gained a great deal in strength since 1951, and she imbues la Tosca with natural and unforced authority, remembering that Tosca is capable of great tenderness; she is never, ever, a caricature of an ill-tempered diva. Vocally, Tebaldi is supple and even throughout, with high notes actually sounding smoother and better supported here than on the earlier recording. Electing to sing (as written) the famous lines in Act Two ("Voglio vederlo" and even "E avanti a lui tremava tutta Roma"), the soprano nevertheless offers a more vibrant and passionate Tosca than previously. The "Vissi d'arte" is an eloquent understatement of grief, sung with sensitivity and fullness of sound, and the two love duets are ecstatically performed.

The crucial encounters with Scarpia are vast improvements over the first recording, mainly because George London's villain is considerably more menacing than Mascherini's. London's voice lacked velvet, and his singing was often unidiomatic in this music, but his rough-hewn, surly villain is a valid if not truly first-rate performance. Mario Del Monaco's Mario is romantic and predictably charismatic, with the tenor amply matching Tebaldi's self-assurance in their love music, while acquitting himself admirably in his two arias. Del Monaco's high Cs in the "Vittoria" trio in the second act are spine-tingling.

Molinari-Pradelli could have helped the performance were his tempi less ponderous, but even the lack of vitality in his conducting does not pose a serious hindrance to the fiery work of the three principals.

It is a little sad that Tebaldi has not redone *Tosca* on records since 1958, for in recent years her Tosca has taken on even greater dramatic force, often with little difficulty on high notes. Those who have access to tapes of Tebaldi's Metropolitan *Toscas* from the 1960s (for example, her March 1964 performance with Gobbi and Corelli, or an April 1969 performance with Domingo and Colzani) will note the development of what had always been one of Tebaldi's key roles into an absolute tour de force of vocalism and acting.

PUCCINI: *IL TRITTICO*

Il Tabarro: The brooding passions of Puccini's score are well served on this recording. Tebaldi is in sumptuous voice as Giorgetta. Furthermore, her characterization of the unhappy young woman is one of her best. Although Giorgetta has no aria to sing, Tebaldi succeeds in creating a musically and dramatically well-defined personality in her long duet with Del Monaco (as Luigi) and in her scene with Merrill (Michele). These two gentlemen are in good form as well, with Merrill being a particularly sympathetic Michele. Del Monaco sounds more mature than is ideal for the youth of twenty that he portrays, but he makes his music ring true. The supporting cast is uniformly good and Gardelli's conducting of the Orchestra of the Maggio Musicale Fiorentino is thoughtful and provocative.

Suor Angelica. In the role of the gentle, tormented little nun, Puccini made taxing demands on the soprano. Tebaldi, in fine voice, performs the music with ease, relishing the opportunity for dramatic confrontation that Puccini provided in the scene with Angelica's old Aunt, the Princess, superbly portrayed here by Simionato. Angelica's major aria, "Senza n'mamma tu sei morto o bimbo" is exquisitely sung, with the real pathos of the dramatic moment unencumbered by any elements of the sheerly bathetic. In the upper register, Tebaldi has rarely seemed more easy of sound, making this one of her very finest recordings.

Gianni Schicchi. This sparkling comedy is Puccini's one work in which the soprano does not dominate. Lauretta's role consists of very little more than the thrice familiar aria "O mio babbino caro." Tebaldi sings this with grace and warmth, qualities which along with the basic beauty of her voice, make this a satisfying rendition of the little aria. Otherwise, the performance is distinguished by Fernando Corena's manic Schicchi and Gardelli's effervescent direction.

PUCCINI: *TURANDOT*

That the first Tebaldi *Turandot* (the London-Decca set) is less worth owning (at least, as one's sole recording of Puccini's last opera) than her second one on RCA is entirely due to the lack of distinction of London's Turandot, Inge Borkh. For Tebaldi brought to her earlier Liù an innocence of characterization and an April-fresh tone that she does not surpass on the later RCA performance.Tebaldi's handling on this earlier set of "Signore ascolta" and, especially, the slave girl's death scene encompasses some of the most affecting singing that the soprano has ever done on records. Then too, there is a celestial *pianissimo* on Liù's Act One line "un di, nella reggia mi hai sorriso." Other than for Tebaldi's contribution, this set is notable only for the clarion if somewhat narcissistic Calàf sung by Mario Del Monaco. Borkh's performance of the title role is well-intentioned but lacking in musical excitement and marred by some very edgy high notes. Nicola Zaccaria is a steadfast Timur, and Alberto Erede leads the Santa Cecilia orchestra and chorus with vigor but without ultimate poetic imagination.

The RCA set, recorded in 1959, must rank as one of the most opulently sung recordings of any opera yet to be released, for Tebaldi's Liù was flanked by the incomparable Turandot of Birgit Nilsson and the equally fine Calàf of Jussi Bjoerling. Tebaldi's voice sounds larger and more powerful here than in the London set made some four years earlier, but she controls her volume of sound with utmost skill, singing with remarkable smoothness of tone. She is able to command lovely *pianissimi* here, too. This Liù is a shade more womanly and passionate than the maiden portrayed by the soprano on the first recording. Erich Leindorf's powerful conducting ignites soloists as well as the Rome Opera orchestra and chorus, making this *Turandot* a rewarding experience for the listener.

VERDI: *AIDA*

Aïda paired Tebaldi for the first time on records with Mario Del Monaco, with whom she sang this opera on the occasion of her North American debut in San Francisco in 1950. Here Tebaldi is in bright and generous voice, performing Aïda's music with assurance and an evergrowing sense of authority. "Ritorna vincitor," compared to the earlier recording of the aria, is far more forceful dramatically, and, while the first assay was by no means musically tentative, the performance in the complete recording reveals further mastery of expression of the text and a heightened control of vocal dynamics. Chest tones are knowingly used, while the top notes flow freely.

"O patria mia" is characterized by effortless *pianissimi*, delicacy of phrasing, and silken high notes. Indeed, the entire Nile Scene is quite rousingly sung, with Aldo Protti a forceful and musical Amonasro and Del Monaco providing a stentorian account of Radames's music.

The Amneris on this recording is Ebe Stignani, one of the finest Italian singers of the 1030s and 1940s. Stignani offers a kind of matronly authority and steely, powerful tone that contrasts strikingly with Tebaldi's lyric youthfulness in their second act duet. There, Tebaldi's anguished "Pietà ti prenda del mio dolore" is countered by the awesomely forceful "Trema, vil schiava" of Stignani. Clearly here Aïda is at the mercy of a formidable rival.

The monaural recording makes less of the intricacies of the Triumphal Scene than stereo sets, of course, but the voices are excellently captured, with Tebaldi's exquisite cadenza capping the "Ma tu re, tu signore possente" ensemble.

The Tomb Scene finds Del Monaco in a more reflective state than usual, and he blends handsomely with the soprano's ecstatic greeting of the angel of death.

VERDI: *AÏDA*

The stereo *Aïda* was one of two recordings Tebaldi made with Herbert von Karajan, at the Vienna State Opera. Less than a totally happy recording session, it is said, it netted an uneven but interesting recording, which featured Carlo Bergonzi as Radames, Giulietta Simionato as Amneris, and Cornell MacNeil as Amonasro.

The soprano was suffering from exhaustion at the time of the recording, and indeed, cancelled concurrent performances of the opera onstage at the State Opera in order to complete the taping. Her high Cs are hard pressed, and a little under pitch, but aside from these blemishes Tebaldi's singing is of her usual standard. The middle range of her voice is in especially fine shape, making for a lovely rendering of the duet with Radames in Act Three, and a highly satisfactory account of "O patria mia" (up to the final phrase, which is marred by the flat high C). Dramatically, Tebaldi is even more poised than on her earlier recording, and the vocal duel with Amneris in Act Two, Scene 1 is immensely exciting, with the two women matching each other in dynamism and heat. In spite of the curiously cold acoustical properties of the recording, Tebaldi has no trouble reaching her usual volume of tone, and her voice soars easily in the Triumphal Scene ensemble. The Tomb Scene provides still another example of the heavenly qualities of Tebaldi's *piano* singing.

Simionato surpasses Stignani (and indeed, everyone else, too!) as Amneris, providing in her affected wickedness the best possible foil for Tebaldi's good-hearted heroine. Her high notes are metallic, but powerfully delivered, and her Judgment Scene is spectacular. Bergonzi is a gentlemanly, dramatically reserved Radames, whose "Celeste Aïda" is appropriately (and uniquely, on records) romantic, as opposed to martial. Through his intelligent musicianship, Bergonzi makes Radames into a more appealing and sympathetic character than he becomes when other tenors bellow his music.

MacNeil offers solid tone as Amonasro, but neither Arnold van Mill nor Corena are in top form as Ramphis and the King, respectively. The Vienna Friends of Music are unsatisfactory as a chorus here, sounding tentative musically and very amateurish in terms of diction. Karajan's heavy, uninvolved tempi throw a damper on the score, which never fully comes alive despite the fine singing by the four principals.

VERDI: *UN BALLO IN MASCHERA*

Tebaldi's most recent complete opera recording again finds her singing a role that she never performed on stage. Amelia, the unhappy wife of Renato, is a character to which Tebaldi is well suited. In the summer of 1970, when this set was made, however, Tebaldi was not in best voice. A definite element of strain pervades her singing, and the high Cs are produced at what evidently was considerable cost.

The soprano had recorded the two arias for Amelia once before on her 1964 recital disc, and while she captures the anguish of Amelia's plight to a greater extent in the later recording, the performance remains vocally inferior. Still, Tebaldi's masterful handling of the music and her terse, personally involved and incisive projection of the text gives her Amelia a depth and a musical integrity that is to be respected. In the crucial second act duet with Riccardo, Tebaldi's voice soars far more freely than in the aria which opens the act, and she makes the most of the opportunities offered her by the composer. The aria "Morrò, ma prima in grazia," despite the basically leaner, harder sound of Tebaldi's voice here, is excitingly, even beautifully performed. Indeed, the vivid characterization, as well as the basic and complete understanding of the kind of singing called for here, even though the soprano is not always able to fulfill the purely vocal requirements, make one doubly sorry that Tebaldi did not sing and record Amelia years earlier!

Tebaldi's colleagues here include Luciano Pavarotti as Riccardo and Sherrill Milnes as Renato. Both gentlemen exhibit their gorgeous voices freely—and neither sings with a great deal of conviction or authority. Regina Resnik is a very tired-sounding Ulrica while Helen Donath sings Oscar prettily but with little *brio*. Bruno Bartoletti conducts.

VERDI: *DON CARLOS*

Don Carlos recorded in the summer of 1965, was the first complete opera recording Tebaldi made after her one-year absence from singing in 1963-64. Of course, she had already made the recital disc released in January 1965, and had made any number of appearances at the Metropolitan and elswhere in such roles as Mimi, Tosca, Desdemona, and Amelia in *Simon Boccanegra,* but this complex, all-star recording of a role that she had never sung on stage was one of the major projects of Tebaldi's reborn career.

Although the DGG five act Don Carlos set had been available for several years, the cast London-Decca assembled for this venture made it an important and eagerly awaited release. In addition to Tebaldi, the cast included Bergonzi in the title role, Bumbry as Eboli, Fischer-Dieskau as Rodrigo, Ghiaurov as Philip II, Talvela as the Grand Inquisitor. Solti conducted the Royal Opera Orchestra and Chorus.

For those accustomed to the sound of Tebaldi's voice on early recordings, this *Don Carlos* must have come as a surprise. The timbre is leaner, perhaps a little darker, and definitely more mature. If Elisabetta's first phrase "Ah, come stanco son" ("Ah, how tired I am") and Tebaldi's world-weary rendering of it suggest one of opera's more stately heroines rather than the innocent princess of the Fontainebleau scene, the soprano lightens her tone in the ensuing duet with Don Carlos, enjoying, as it were, Elisabetta's only tranquil moment in the opera.

Tebaldi's conception of Elisabetta is fraught with a sense of impending disaster. She captures the agony of the queen's situation, communicating this to the listener with rich shading of text and notes. From a purely vocal standpoint, the edge that had begun to appear in Tebaldi's high notes is obvious, as in the Act Two, Scene 2 duet with Carlos and *forte* singing in the upper reaches is apt to be steely in quality. Yet in softer passages, particularly those associated with Elisabetta's grief—that heartrending melody in the Cabinet

Scene quartet, to cite one example, or the lovers' final leave-taking—Tebaldi is splendidly limpid in sound, caressing each phrase with her wonted sweetness of voice. Elisabetta and Eboli, in the version of the opera generally performed today, have only a few seconds in which they square off with one another at the end of Act Four, Scene 1, when the Queen banishes the Princess to a convent. But here Tebaldi's regal fury matches Grace Bumbry's impassioned remorse.

Act Five, of course, more or less "belongs" to the soprano, who opens it with the difficult "Tu che le vanità conoscesti del mondo." Here Tebaldi seems more in command than on her recital disc recording of that aria a year or so earlier. Although her handling of this music is surely not effortless, Tebaldi imparts solidity of line and considerable authority to the piece. As a total performance, Elisabetta does not stand out as Tebaldi's most impressive achievement, and one wishes that she had recorded the part earlier. However, though her voice is less fresh here than in other recordings, Tebaldi's affecting characterization and adroit musicianship—not to mention many stunning moments—make her an always interesting and often commanding figure.

Turning to Tebaldi's colleagues, this *Don Carlos* is further distinguished by the impeccable title role performance of Carlo Bergonzi, who imbues every phrase with elegance and gorgeous sound, the bravura work of Grace Bumbry as Eboli, the powerfully sung and frighteningly acted King Philip of Nicolai Ghiaurov, the equally imposing Grand Inquisitor of Martti Talvela, and the incisive conducting of Sir Georg Solti. Of the principal singers, only Dietrich Fischer-Dieskau seems badly miscast. Singing with musical precision and an admittedly handsome tone, the baritone is too reserved as Rodrigo and his Italian diction lacks true ease.

VERDI: *LA FORZA DEL DESTINO*

This is not only one of the soprano's finest individual performances, but the total effect of the recording is to make the listener aware that the 1950s in Italy was a true golden age of singing. Certainly, it would be hard to imagine a more gifted cast—Tebaldi as Leonora, Del Monaco as Alvaro, Bastianini as Don Carlo, Siepi as Padre Guardiano, Corena as Melitone, and Simionato as Preziosilla—and conductor Molinari-Pradelli, not often more than a *routinier*, here molds these forces into a powerful account of a great and complex score.

Tebaldi is in perfect form here, with creamy top notes devoid of any metallic edge, silken control of the middle register, and thrilling chest tones that are not exaggerated. "Me pellegrina ed orfana" is very beautifully sung, while the agitation and suffering that Tebaldi conveys in the rest of the scene is precisely the sort of instinctive characterization lacking in the *Trovatore* performance.

The Convent Scene might possibly be the finest singing Tebaldi ever committed to disc—secure, powerful, full of conviction, dynamically varied and pristine in tone . . . sides 3 and 4 of this set are eminently cherishable. Tebaldi's "Pace, pace mio dio" is similarly eloquent. The soprano's upper register is singularly free in this performance, and here evident identification with Leonora's plight makes for work that is as interesting histrionically as it is superlative musically. Mario Del Monaco is in fine voice, sounding pushed only in his very first entrance, but he soon recovers, and his duet with Tebaldi in the opening scene is marked by singing of high order indeed. Bastianini is equally good, thrilling the listener with his silken, dark voice. The tenor-baritone duets are outstandingly performed. Cesare Siepi is a rather youthful-sounding Guardiano, but his musicianship and mellow singing make up for a certain lack of authority in the part. His duet with Tebaldi in the Convent Scene is a recording to prize most highly. Simionato is a vivid Preziosilla and Corena an enormously amusing Melitone. The performance is uncut, except for a few bars of the baritone's third act cabaletta, and the performance, some fifteen years after its release, towers over other recorded *Forzas*.

VERDI: *GIOVANNA D'ARCO* (Pirated Recording)

One of Tebaldi's most fascinating performances is captured on this pirated set. Recorded in Venice at the Teatro La Fenice in 1951, it reveals the soprano in her early prime. *Giovanna d'Arco,* composed several years before *Traviata,* is the earliest Verdian role Tebaldi has ever sung. In this early opera, Verdi's style still owes much to Donizetti and even Bellini, but Tebaldi copes adequately, at times even brilliantly, with the florid vocal line. Moreover, the warmness and richness of her voice is in itself remarkable; Tebaldi seldom, if ever, sang with more beauty of sound than that which she manifests here.

Giovanna, as befits her status as heroine of this work, has two important arias, duets with the tenor and the baritone, and a rather remarkable death scene in which she seemingly returns from the other world to vocally soar heavenward during the finale.

However absurd Solero's libretto may be, Tebaldi establishes Giovanna as a forthright personality and thus histrionically as well as vocally makes her the center of attention. Highlights of the performance are "Sempre all' alba," which is sung with a proper mix of ethereal tone and human passion, and the duet with the dauphin which follows directly afterward. Giovanna's death scene, which in some ways suggests those of *Traviata, Forza,* and even *Aïda,* is also excellently wrought, with no hint of saccharine sentiment.

Also of great interest on this recording is the dauphin sung by Carlo Bergonzi, who had switched from baritone to tenor only months before this performance was given. Since this recording was made, Bergonzi's voice has rung out with more confidence and his musicianship has become more refined, but his vigorous, attractive singing as evidenced here still does him proud.

Rolando Panerai is the highly competent Giacomo, Giovanna's father and the opera's chief villain, while Alfredo

Simonetto leads the Fenice orchestra and chorus with flair, if little subtlety.

In the end, what impresses one most in regard to this recording is Tebaldi's handling of Giovanna's *bel canto* vocal line, leaving the listener to expect that, had she been so inclined, Tebaldi could have become a true dramatic soprano *d'agilitã* and might, in fact, have become a Norma to be reckoned with. Obviously, her own interests led Tebaldi to the later works of Verdi and the operas of Puccini and the other *verismo* composers. However when indulging in a game of guessing what might have been, this recording supplies evidence that Tebaldi could have sung certain heroines of Donizetti and Bellini with great success.

VERDI: *OTELLO*

This early *Otello* is graced by the pliant ease of Tebaldi's singing, her freedom in the upper register, and her ability to float *pianissimi* (the beautiful effect of which can be heard most notably at the end of the "Ave Maria").

Dramatically, Tebaldi offers a demure portrayal for the most part, although passion and outrage are certainly in evidence in the "Dio ti giocondi" and the ensemble which caps the third act. Indeed, Tebaldi's rendition of the section comes close to being absolutely definitive.

Mario Del Monaco makes a virile and charismatic Moor, but his characterization lacks detail. Aldo Protti is a subdued Iago, but Piero di Palma is an excellent Cassio. Alberto Erede's conducting is crisp and incisive, however he does not delve deeply into the score.

VERDI: *OTELLO*

The second London *Otello*, also made at the Vienna State Opera with von Karajan, but this time utilizing the State Opera Chorus, is a generally impressive performance. Von Karajan, often not entirely idiomatic in his direction of Italian opera, here leads a strong and meticulously detailed

Otello, his tempi grandly imposing but never too heavy, making the great ensemble in Act Three the musical-dramatic high point of the opera. Karajan elected to include in this recording the ballet music Verdi composed for Paris, a decision that is academically interesting but one which dissipates some of the tension building up in the Otello-Desdemona encounter and the scene with Cassio that precedes the ballet.

In addition to Tebaldi, London reengaged several other members of the cast of the monaural *Otello:* Del Monaco in the title role, Protti as Iago, de Palma as Cassio, and even Corena as Lodovico. Tebaldi's work on the second recording is notable for its tonal richness and increased emotional involvement with the character. Thus the "Giã nella notte densa" is serene and almost regal in its delivery, but by the time the Moor grows menacing in "Dio ti giocondi," Tebaldi adds a palpable sense of surprise and then fear to her singing. Desdemona's bitter "Guarda le prime lagrime" is sung with an unsurpassable communication of broken pride and despair. Tebaldi's voice soars clearly through the ensemble, delving intensely into the confusion of feelings in Desdemona at that moment.

VERDI: *LA TRAVIATA*

London-Decca's monaural *Traviata,* now available on the budget Richmond label, surrounds Tebaldi with a sadly lackluster cast, including Gianni Poggi, who sings Alfredo with frequent lapses of intonation and stylistic insensitivity, and Aldo Protti, who is little more than adequate as the elder Germont. Under Molinari-Pradelli's stolid and uninspired direction, the performance seldom takes wing.

Tebaldi, as in her Met performances of the opera, elects to transpose downward the "Sempre libera," which sounds effortful in any case, but in virtually every other passage impresses with the exceptional purity of her singing and the simple nobility of her characterization. In particular, Violetta's opening phrases in the third act ensemble are exquisitely sung, as is the entire fourth act. The great duet with

Germont remains earthbound whenever Protti sings, but Tebaldi's performance there is luminescent.

VERDI: *IL TROVATORE*

Tebaldi has never sung the *Trovatore* Leonora onstage, although she programmed the first act aria "Tacea la notte placida" in a number of her recitals. She did, however, record the complete opera for London-Decca in 1957, in the distinguished company of Mario Del Monaco as Manrico, Giulietta Simionato as Azucena, and Giorgio Tozzi as Ferrando, as well as Ugo Savarese as di Luna. Alberto Erede conducted the Orchestra and Chorus of L'Accademia di Santa Cecilia.

This recording was the first to utilize virtually the entire score, reinstating such usual cuts as the second verse of Leonora's first act cabaletta "Di tale armor," the full ending to the trio that closes the act, repeats in the duet for Manrico and Azucena in Act Two, Scene 1, both verses of "Di quella pira," and the lovely cabaletta to the soprano's fourth act aria, "Tu vedrai." This recording set a trend for uncut *Trovatores,* and even the Metropolitan currently asks that its Leonoras be prepared to perform the fourth act in its entirety.

Turning to the performance itself, it must be said that Tebaldi's Leonora, like the character itself, is a bit problematical. Vocally, the soprano finds the fioratura of "Di tale amor" a little fatiguing, and sounds slightly breathy and pressured in this number. Elsewhere, Tebaldi succeeds in purely musical terms, with a particularly thoughtful and demure "Tacea la notte placida." The fourth act, too, is quite handsomely sung, with "D'amor sull'ali" sounding limpid and velvety (the "trill" at the end of the latter piece is ersatz but acceptable). The "Miserere" is strikingly sung by soprano and tenor (the chorus is crisp throughout the performance) and Tebaldi's rendering of "Tu vedrai" must have been a revelation to those previously unfamiliar with this piece. *Trovatore* is one opera in which the tenor and soprano, though lovers, have no extended scene together (besides the "Miserere" during which they are physically separated), while the soprano's only big duet is sung with the baritone. In this case, the substandard dry wheeze of Savarese prevents Tebaldi from entering into a true musical collaboration here. Her part in the scene is performed with delicacy of phrasing (the grace notes are exceptionally well handled) but the full effect of this dashingly melodramatic scene is not realized. Elsewhere in ensembles, Tebaldi ranges from the slightly steely in tone (first act trio) to the heavenly endowed in the second act finale (her leave-taking of Inez in the opening moments of the scene is especially fine), while the soprano's handling of Leonora's death is similarly excellent. All that is really lacking in her performance is the complete identification with the character that one finds in Tebaldi's Puccini heroines, and in such Verdian roles as Violetta, Desdemona, Aïda, or the *Forza* Leonora. Granted, the *Trovatore* heroine is rather pallid . . . always sad (if ultimately noble), and usually passive. Leonora offers little to spark the dramatic imagination. However, Tebaldi might have been able, in future years to delve more deeply into Leonora's pysche than she did in this recording.

Before moving on, it ought to be noted that Giulietta Simionato's Azucena is vocally impeccable, and dramatically the most exciting that I have ever heard; that Del Monaco's headstrong and resonant Manrico is a little lacking in the finer graces that make, say, Bjoerling, so unforgettable in the role, but his "Di quella pira" epitomizes Verdian excitement; and that Tozzi is a youthful and full-voiced Ferrando. Erede's conducting is more lively than his general standard, and he adds real dramatic thrust to the ensembles and climactic passages. Tebaldi's difficulty with "Di tale amor," though, may be due in part to Erede's taking that piece at too rapid a tempo.

RECITALS

OPERATIC RECITAL

Recalling the early years of her career recently, Tebaldi noted that, "While I had, of course, been singing major roles all over Italy for several years, I was not well known outside of Italy until I made my first recordings for Decca [London in the United States] in 1947. I was invited to Geneva where I recorded arias from *Aïda* ["Ritorna vincitor"], *Faust* [The Ballad of the King of Thule and the Jewel Song in Italian,] *Tosca* ["Vissi d'arte"], *Manon Lescaut* ["In quelle trine morbide"], *Il Trovatore* ["Tacea la notte placida"], and *Madama Butterfly* ["Un bel di"]. These recordings, first released as singles on 78 rpm discs, and later as *Operatic Recital Number 1* on LPs, brought me my first recognition outside of Italy." This disc, unfortunately, has been deleted from the catalogue, perhaps because it was not recorded stereophonically. However, those lucky enough to own it already, or those who manage to obtain a copy in a back-issue record shop will attest to the beauty of the singing. In retrospect, the most interesting piece on the disc is the *Faust* excerpt, for although the opera was a vehicle for some of the young artist's early major successes, it was a role that Tebaldi never performed outside of Italy, and never sang in French. If the trill in the "Jewel Song" is not quite authentic, the vocalism is warm and, of course, cannily phrased, the projection of the text excellent, and the tone as vibrant and youthful as might be wished.

Of the five remaining arias comprising this first series of recordings the most striking is "Un bel di," sung with clarity, power, and a sure sense of the character of the abandoned Japanese bride. The *Tosca* and *Manon Lescaut* arias are lustrously performed and pale only against the heightened enunciation and authority of the complete recordings of the two operas made years later. The two Verdi pieces are similarly well sung, with the *Trovatore* aria seeming ever so slightly more polished than the *Aïda* aria.

SONG RECITALS

Although unavailable at the present time, these two discs, made in the early 1950s with Giorgio Favoretto at the piano, offer Tebaldi in a variety of attractive and impressively sung songs, with an occasional aria added for good measure.

The first disc finds a sumptuously sung "Leggiadri occhi

belli," and a dainty, girlish rendition of Scarlatti's "Le violette." Handel's opera *Giulio Cesare* in which Tebaldi sang the role of Cleopatra, is represented by the aria "pianger̀o la sorte mia," in a pensive, lush, but rather slowly paced manner, More idiomatically presented are such pieces as Rossini's waltz *La Promessa,* a delightful bit of fluff that the composer created during his Paris retirement, and two pieces by Bellini, "Dolente imagine di fille mia" and "Vanne, o rosa fortunata." Verdi's *Stornello,* sung with the properly mischievous spirit, but at a tempo that may strike listeners as overly cautious . . . Tebaldi sings this one at a much faster clip these days!

SONG RECITAL NO. 2

Highlights of the second disc include Tebaldi's youthful, delightful handling of the Rossini "cycle" *La Regata Veneziana,*" three songs which have remained favorite concert pieces throughout her career; two more Bellini songs, "Vaga luna che inargenti" and "Per pietā, bell'idol mio"; and an incredibly beautiful rendering of a simple and touching Mascagni song "M'ama, non m'ama," in whose measures Tebaldi finds means to show all the insecurity and delicious self-torments of a young girl in love. Two Mozart pieces, "Ridente la calma" (K. 152) and "Un moto di gioa" (K. 579) are sung with radiant tone. The disc includes, among other, lighter pieces, "A vuchella" by Tosti, which is also still a frequent visitor to Tebaldi's concert repertoire.

THE ARTISTRY OF RENATA TEBALDI

This budget-priced disc, available in the United States on Everest, is comprised of arias recorded by the soprano for RAI early in her career. With the exception of one piece, "Deh vieni, non tardar," Tebaldi has recorded every aria here at least once for London-Decca. The Mozart aria is attractively vocalized, Tebaldi suggesting a fuller voiced, less sprightly Susanna than one usually hears, yet her delicacy of phrasing and warm enunciation are most pleasureable. "Addio del passato" is perhaps sung even better here than on the complete recording and the accounts of "O patria mia" and the "Willow Song" are typically good. Mimi's two arias are also present, sung with freshness of sound and interpretive sympathy. Three *verismo* pieces, "Ebbene, ne andrō lontano" from *La wally,* "L'altre notte" from *Mefistofele* and "La mamma morta" from *Chenier* round out the recital, which represents an excellent survey of the early work of the soprano. Most of the Decca-London recordings of these arias carry more dramatic authority, and indeed, the British firm's recorded sound is vastly superior to Everest-Cetra's. However, the disc is worth its nominal price.

TEBALDI IN STEREO

This album, the electronically reprocessed descendant of a mono set known simply as *Tebaldi Operatic Recital No. 3,* offers Tebaldi in a variety of operatic excerpts, including several from roles that she performed only rarely if at all. Commencing with the Countess's two arias from *Le Nozze di Figaro,* the album includes the two familiar soprano arias from *Adriana Lecouvreur,* "Flammen perdonami" from Mascagni's *Lodoletta,* "Selva opaca" from *Guillaume Tell,* "Ne mai dunque avrō la pace" from *La Wally,* and two practically unknown pieces from the Jesuit Refice's opera *Cecilia,* in which the leading role is the martyred patron saint of music.

"Porgi amore," in its languor and wistfulness, finds Tebaldi's voice a lovely means of expression. "Dove sono" is sung with some strain in the final measures, however. The *Adriana* pieces are admirably sung, perhaps with even a smoother tone than on the complete recording which followed several years later. The *Wally* piece is strongly performed, although the 1968 recording is even more dramatic! The "Flammen perdonami" is my personal favorite of the pieces on this disc, sung with complete security of production, meltingly warm tone, and a firm but not overdone sense of pathos of the scene in question (the soprano character is freezing to death in a blizzard while the tenor hosts a ball indoors!)

"Selva opaca" is sung with a fitting sense of urgency and evenly produced, opulent high notes. As for the two *Cecilia* excerpts, they are musically undistinguished, striking this listener as a rehash of Puccini, composed without the latter's genius. Still, Tebaldi lets her voice soar freely through this music, which includes the actual martyrdom of the poor saint. These performances feature the Orchestra and Chorus L'Accademia di Santa Cecilia, under Erede's benign and rather pallid direction.

AN EVENING AT THE CHICAGO LYRIC OPERA

This 1957 release, now deleted from the London catalogue, was comprised of excerpts from a live benefit concert at the Chicago Lyric Opera. Tebaldi, Simionato, and Bastianini, conducted by Georg Solti, appear on the disc (only London-Decca artists were recorded that night). Tebaldi sings two pieces that she recorded in the studio, "La mamma morta" from *Chenier* and "L'altra notte" from *Mefistofele.* The Giordano aria is particularly successful, but the disc's main interest is Tebaldi's singing (in Italian) of Tatiana's "Letter Scene" from *Eugene Onegin.* The soprano performed this role at La Scala with success, and was invited by Bing to create the role in his English-language revival which opened the Metropolitan Opera's 1957-58 season. Not wishing to relearn the role in English, Tebaldi declined, and Lucine Amara opened the season instead that year.

Tebaldi's Tatiana seems emotionally developed beyond her years, as the soprano brings a womanly passion (quite appropriate to the situation) to her work here. Her voice flows freely, soaring brilliantly to the top of the scale in a performance which, fired by Solti's intense conducting, justifies the black market price one is forced to pay for the disc these days, should one be lucky enough to come across it.

A special bonus is the *Gioconda* duet "L'amo come il fulgor di creato," in which Tebaldi demonstrates the proper feeling and almost as much vocal weight as she brought to the role in full performance a decade later, while Simionato sings with molten tones. How interesting, parenthetically, it is to find

Solti conducting these excerpts from a repertoire that he is not usually associated with. The era's consummate Wagnerian shows firm command of the late nineteenth century Italian (and Russian) idioms.

OPERATIC ARIAS

This collection of arias was the first record made by the soprano in 1964 after her year away from singing, and the results were eagerly awaited. With the exception of the aria from *Cavalleria Rusticana,* Tebaldi had not yet recorded any of the material on this collection, although she eventually recorded *Don Carlos Gioconda,* and *Ballo* complete.

The first side, devoted entirely to Verdi, opens with "Tu che le vanità." If the high notes are marked by steeliness, and the tone generally less opulent than one had been accustomed to, the overall impression is that of poised, highly professional musicianship.

The two *Ballo* arias are vigorously sung, and the *Giovanna d'Arco* excerpt, "Sempre all'alba," is fresh voiced and appealing. (Hearing this piece ought to stimulate listeners to search for the 1951 pirate recording of this opera with Tebaldi and Carlo Bergonzi, discussed earlier.) The second side is made up of *verismo* and late nineteenth century operatic gems. It seems as if Tebaldi had once considered singing the title role in *Turandot.* The sample found here, "In questa reggia," is quite brilliant, with secure if somewhat metallic high Cs and elsewhere a refreshingly tender account of the forces that made the Princess into an icy monster. According to a reliable source, no less an artist than Joan Sutherland has modelled her recent (recorded) Turandot interpretation on the Tebaldi recording of this aria. The "Suicidio" points to the exciting *Gioconda* to come some three years later, with increasingly prominent chest tones and a striking command of the tessitura of the piece. "Voi lo sapete" is less richly sung than on the complete performance, but is intensely etched by the soprano. By contrast the "Sogno di Doretta" from Puccini's *La Rondine* offers a moment of warm sentimentality, although here, too, some of the top tones are disappointingly harsh. The aria, though, is sung with such lavishness of feeling that despite this flaw it emerges as one of the most memorable components of the disc. The final selection, "Esser madre è un inferno," from Cilea's *L'Arlesiana* is the least inspired music found on the recording, but Tebaldi sings idiomatically and with a sense of character. Anton Guadagno offers excellent direction throughout the disc.

TEBALDI FESTIVAL

Issued in the fall of 1969, this two-disc set, complete with a booklet containing dozens of photographs of the soprano and laudatory essays by Terry McEwen and Francis Robinson, is especially geared to the Tebaldi fan. Still, apart from the packaging, the album offers an interesting program, and one that is sung quite impressively as well. Side 1 contains four Wagnerian excerpts, sung in Italian. Both of Elisabeth's major arias from *Tannhäuser* are included. "Dich, teure halle" is sung with ecstatic abandon, and "Elisabeth's Prayer" and "Elsa's Dream" from *Lohengrin* each boast Tebaldi's tone at its sweetest and most attractive. Her Liebestod is an extraordinary blending of Tebaldi's own Italian romanticism with the Wagnerian variety. The result is musically polished and very moving.

The second side contains half a dozen French arias, also in Italian . . . the linear notes state that Tebaldi chose to sing in translation in order to be able to color each word with proper emphasis and not have to worry about pronunciation.

This section begins with *Carmen*'s Habanera and Card Scene. The former piece comes off as slightly coy, but the latter excerpt is riveting. Next come the heroine's second act pieces from *Samson et Dalila,* "Amour, viens aidez ma faiblesse" and "Mon coeur s'ouvre a ta voix," which Tebaldi uses to explore and exploit her chest register. The last two arias are from Massenet's *Manon,* an opera which Tebaldi studied and intended to sing on stage. "Adieu, notre petite table" is most affecting, while the St. Sulpice excerpt "Ne-c'est plus ma main" is the single most memorable aria on the whole recital. Complete identification with character is present, and the soft, tender phrases of the music are treated to artistry at its very best. Anton Guadagno conducts the New Philharmonia tastefully.

The second disc, in which Tebaldi and the same orchestra are conducted by Richard Bonynge, commences with an authoritative "Ritorna vincitor" in which the soprano displays still further mastery of the drama, if her previous recordings reveal her in fresher voice. Other pieces on this disc are Musetta's Waltz, knowingly sung, and a pleasant interpretation of "La regata veneziana." The last side offers six warmly sung "encore" numbers, the last of which is a captivating performance, in captivating English, of Rodgers' and Hammerstein's "If I Loved You", which has become Tebaldi's favorite encore in her U.S. and London concerts.

Again, although the *Tebaldi Festival* is obviously directed to Tebaldiani tried and true, the repertoire and performances are entirely valid, and many of the individual selections are extremely distinguished. One cannot find a more lovely Elsa in *Lohengrin* in any language, and the *Tannhäuser* excerpts, particularly the prayer, are worthy of comparison to such lyric Wagnerians as Rethberg or Flagstad.

A CHRISTMAS FESTIVAL

In line with the fad of popular operatic artists issuing discs of Christmas carols and associated music, Tebaldi's London-Decca disc was released in time for Christmas 1971, although it was recorded a couple of years earlier. The album features Christmas carols popular in Europe and the United States, including "Silent Night," "O Holy Night," and "What Child Is This?", each of which is sung in English ("Silent Night" is also sung in French and German). Among the Italian language selections are Schubert's "Mille cherubini in coro" and "Tu scendi della stella," while the Bach-Gounod "Ave Maria" and Brahms' Lullaby, sung in somewhat tentative German, are also present. The disc begins and ends, strangely, with the same "take" of "Adeste Fidelis." Anton Guadagno conducts the New Philharmonia Orchestra and the Ambrosian Singers provide intermittent choral support. The orchestrations are soupy and Guadagno's tempi are pleasantly sentimental. Tebaldi is in delightful voice in such numbers as "O Holy Night" and the Brahms' Lullaby. The latter, however, with its "Muzak" orchestration, sounds synthetic, despite the warmth of Tebaldi's singing. The Italian carols are charming, and "O Holy Night" is really quite impressive. The polyglot "Silent Night" is also treasurable, while "Adeste Fidelis" is slightly overwhelmed by Tebaldi's voice at full power. In all, this is hardly Tebaldi's most memorable set, but it is appealing all the same.

TEBALDI IN CONCERT

This 1972 recording, featuring Tebaldi with Richard Bonynge at the piano, preserves a number of the songs included on the soprano's recent concert programs. For some reason, Donizetti's sparkling "Me voglio fa'na casa," which Tebaldi performed with greater success in the actual concerts, is chosen to open the disc, although in terms of her singing, it is the weakest piece on the record. Once past this somewhat strained beginning, the soprano offers some lovely *piano* singing in "Ah cessate di piagarmi," "Ma preso alla sua ragna," and several other pieces. A Zandonai song, "L'assiuolo," is a haunting original piece, strikingly sung. The remainder of the program is pleasant enough to listen to, but there is a certain element of caution in Tebaldi's singing which, coupled with the rather lightweight nature of most of the songs, makes the recording less than fully satisfactory. Bonynge's accompaniment is sympathetic and assured.

GREAT LOVE DUETS WITH FRANCO CORELLI

Tebaldi's most recent recording for London-Decca, released in 1973, unites her for the first time on discs with Franco Corelli. (The tenor had been signed to record *La Gioconda* with Tebaldi, but he withdrew and was replaced by Bergonzi.) This disc offers the two artists, who have sung together so often, in a variety of pieces including two tenor-mezzo duets. While neither singer can truly be said to be in top form in this recording, the long duet from Zandonai's *Francesca da Rimini* comes off very well indeed; Tebaldi spins languid phrases and moves through the music with skill and ease, and Corelli seems more sympathetic than elsewhere on this disc. The *Manon Lescaut* excerpt, "Tu, tu amore tu" is vocally dry and doesn't stand up well next to Tebaldi's complete recording of the opera. The brief encounter between Adriana Lecouvreur and Maurizio in the second act of the Cilea opera finds Tebaldi in rather good voice, although Corelli here bleats unmercifully.

The *Aïda* excerpt is exciting in that one gets an idea of what Tebaldi's Amneris would be like. Her ideas are unfailingly right, but her voice sounds uncharacteristically dry here, and she indulges in too many register breaks.

The *Gioconda* duet for Enzo and Laura is an interesting footnote to Tebaldi's *Gioconda*, whose music she finds more congenial. Anton Guadagno conducts the Orchestre de la Suisse Romande, in what must be deemed the soprano's least satisfactory recording.

THREE SCENES FROM *FAUST* AND EXCERPTS FROM THE *VERDI REQUIEM* AND ROSSINI'S *STABAT MATER* (Pirated Recording)

Those enterprising recording pirates who call themselves Penzance Records (an interesting pun, considering the trouble Gilbert & Sullivan had with "pirated" versions of their operettas!) offer a disc available in England as well as the United States containing three scenes from *Faust*, sung in Italian at the San Carlo in 1950 with Tebaldi as Marguerite, Mario Filippeschi as Faust, Italo Tajo as Mephisto, and Ugo Savarese as Valentine. The sound is quite poor, with much scratchy surface noise, through which can often be discerned Tebaldi singing sweetly as Marguerite. Her work has considerable bite, not only in the Church Scene, but in the excerpt that follows, Valentine's death. After her brother expires, Tebaldi as Marguerite begins to laugh quite madly, a most effective touch, and shows that she was a resourceful actress as far back as 1950. Virtually the entire Prison Scene is included, and Tebaldi acquits herself well there, offering a touching characterization and rich singing. Filippeschi is less than an ideal Faust, but Tajo is a suave-sounding Devil and Savarese shows more vigor than usual in his one short scene. Franco Patane is the conductor.

The second side, mercifully in far better sound, offers excerpts from a 1950 Requiem performance led by Toscanini. The "Ricordare," "Agnus Dei," and "Libera me" are excitingly performed by Tebaldi and Fedora Barbieri, making one long for a complete recording of this performance. No details as to other soloists or the origin of the performance are provided.

The final selection is Rossini's "Inflammatus," with Tebaldi supported by an unidentified orchestra, chorus and conductor; the date given is 1954. Her voice is captured reasonably well here, and her sympathetic performance may be valued even though, again, a complete performance would be preferable.

TEBALDI AND TUCKER IN OPERATIC DUETS
(Pirated Recording)

This 1973 disc, manufactured from tapes of Metropolitan Opera broadcasts between 1958 and 1961, captures both soprano and tenor in luscious form. The disc includes excerpts from *Manon Lescaut* (1958) *La Forza del Destino* (1960), *Andrea Chenier* (1960) and *Simon Boccanegra* (1961). The *Forza* duet from the Prologue represents Tebaldi's last appearance in the role of Leonora, in a performance that took place just one week after Leonard Warren died onstage at the Met in this opera. Unfortunately, this duet is not one of *Forza's* great moments, but the two artists perform most compellingly. Even more impressive are the two duets from *Chenier* (how beautifully Tebaldi shapes the phrase "Erivate possente" in Act Two); the fourth act duet is truly exciting, sung in the original key (one half tone higher than often performed). The two scenes from *Manon Lescaut* ("Tu, tu amore tu" and the first part of Act Four, including "Sola, perduta e abbandonata") are among the most sensually impressive that Tebaldi ever performed. The first act duet from *Boccanegra* represents the only music from the opera that ever found its way onto a Tebaldi disc (complete tapes of the performance circulate, too, of course) and find the soprano in near-top form, sounding just a shade heavy and tired on top.

This recording, capturing the excitement generated by live performances, is a highly desirable souvenir of the work of these two artists, who appeared together frequently in the States but never recorded in the studio together.

Discography

Note: Opera recordings are complete unless otherwise indicated. Recordings marked with an asterisk are no longer available except through dealers specializing in out-of-print recordings.

Operas

Boito, *Mefistofele*
Cavalli, Del Monaco, Siepi, cond. Serafin — 3-London OSA 1307
Highlights — London OS 25083
Highlights, di Stefano, Siepi, cond. Serafin — London OS 26274
Bergonzi, Ghiaurov, cond. Gardelli (Amer. Opera Society, pirate) MRF = 4

Catalani, *La Wally*
Del Monaco, Cappuccilli, Diaz, cond. Cleva — 3-London OSA 1392
Highlights — London OS 26202
Bergonzi, Glossop, Corena, cond. Gardelli (Amer. Opera Society, pirate) (mono only) — MRF = 77

Cilea, *Adriana Lecouvreur*
Simionato, Del Monaco, Fioravanti, cond. Capuana — 3-London OSA 1331
Highlights — London OS 25715

Giordano, *Andrea Chenier*
Del Monaco, Bastianini, cond. Gavazzeni — 3-London OSA 1303
Highlights — London OS 25076
Soler, Savarese, cond. Basile — Everest S 412-2

Giordano, *Fedora*
di Stefano, Sereni, cond. Basile (San Carlo, pirate) (mono only) — MRF = 40

Discography

156 Tebaldi as Gioconda
at the Metropolitan in 1966 (Melançon).

Mascagni, *Cavalleria Rusticana*
Bjoerling, Bastianini, cond. Erede — 2-London OSA 12101

Ponchielli, *La Gioconda*
Horne, Bergonzi, Merrill, cond. Gardelli — 3-London OSA 1388
Highlights — London OS 26162

Puccini, *La Bohème*
D'Angelo, Bergonzi, Bastianini, Siepi, cond. Serafin — 3-London OSA 1208
Highlights — London OS 25201
Gueden, Prandelli, Inghilleri, cond. Erede (mono only) — 3-Richmond RS 62001
Highlights — Richmond R 23034

Puccini, *La Fanciulla del West*
Del Monaco, MacNeil, Tozzi, cond. Capuana — 3-London OSA 1306
Highlights — London OS 25196

Puccini, *Madama Butterfly*
Cossotto, Bergonzi, Sordello, cond. Serafin — 3-London OSA 1314
Highlights — London OS 25084
Rankin, Campora, Inghilleri, cond. Erede (mono only) — 3-Richmond RS 63001
Highlights — Richmond R 23036

Puccini, *Manon Lescaut*
Del Monaco, Boriello, Corena, cond. Molinari-Pradelli — 3-London OSA 1317
Highlights — London OS 25713

Puccini, *Tosca*
Del Monaco, London, Corena, cond. Molinari-Pradelli — 3-London OSA 1210
Highlights — London OS 25218
Campora, Mascherini, Corena, cond. Erede (mono only) — 3-Richmond RS 62001
Highlights — Richmond R 23035

Puccini, *Il Trittico (Il Tabarro, Suor Angelica, Gianni Schicchi)*
Simionato, Del Monaco, Merrill, Corena, cond. Gardelli — 3-London OSA 1364
Il Tabarro — London OSA 1151
Suor Angelica — London OSA 1152
Gianni Schicchi — 3-London OSA 1153

Puccini, *Turandot*
Nilsson, Bjoerling, Tozzi, cond. Leinsdorf — 3-RCA LSC 6149
Highlights — RCA LSC 2539
Borkh, Del Monaco, Zaccaria, cond. Erede — 3-London OSA 1308
Highlights — London OS 25193

Verdi, *Aïda*
Simionato, Bergonzi, MacNeil, cond. Karajan — 3-London OSA 1313
Highlights — London OS 25206

Stignani, Del Monaco, Protti, cond. Erede (mono only) 3-Richmond RS 63002
Highlights Richmond R 23037

Verdi, *Un Ballo in Maschera*
Resnik, Donath, Pavarotti, Milnes, cond. Bartoletti 3-London OSA 1398

Verdi, *Don Carlos*
Bumbry, Bergonzi, Fischer-Dieskau, Ghiaurov, Talvela, cond. Solti 4-London OSA 1432
Highlights London OS 26041

Verdi, *Giovanna d'Arco*
Bergonzi, cond. Simoretto (la Fenice pirate) (mono only) MRF = 90

Verdi, *La Forza del Destino*
Simionato, Del Monaco, Bastianini, Siepi, Corena, cond. Molinari-Pradelli 4-London OSA 1405
Highlights London OS 25701

Verdi, *Otello*
Del Monaco, Protti, cond. Karajan 3-London OSA 1324
Highlights London OS 25701
Del Monaco, Protti, cond. Erede (mono only) 3-Richmond RS 63004

Verdi, *Il Traviata*
Poggi, Protti, cond. Molinari-Pradelli (mono only) 3-Richmond RS 63021

Verdi, *Il Trovatore*
Simionato, Del Monaco, Savarese, cond. Erede 3-London OSA 1304

RECITALS

Operatic Recital
"Ritorna vincitor" (Verdi, *Aïda*); "Roi de Thule," "Jewel Song" (Gounod, *Faust*); "In quelle trine morbide" (Puccini, *Manon Lescaut*); "Vissi d'arte" (Puccini, *Tosca*); "Tacea la notte placida" (Verdi, *Il Trovatore*); "Un bel dĩ" (Puccini, *Madama Butterfly*); cond. Erede (mono only) London 5007

Song Recital
"Leggiadri occhi belli" (anon.); "Le Violette" (Scarlatti); "Piangerõ la sorte mia" (Handel, *Giulio Cesare*); "Lungi dal caro mio bene" (Sarti, *Giulio Sabino*); "La Promessa" (Rossini); "Dolente imagine di fille mia," "Vanne, o rosa fortunata" (Bellini); "Stornello" (Verdi); "Al folto bosco," "Cantava il ruscello," "Sur mar al navicella" (Martucci); "A la barcillunisa" (Favara); "Passo e non ti vedo" (Massetti); "Cantares" (Turina); pianist, Favaretto London 50267

Song Recital No. 2
"Chi vuole innamorarsi" (Scarlatti, *Flavio*); "Caldo sangue" (Scarlatti, *Il Sedicia, Re di Gerusalemme*); "Ah spietato" (Handel, *Amadigi*); "La Regata Veneziana" (Rossini); "Ridente la calma," "Un moto di gioia" (Mozart); "Vaga luna che inargenti," "Per pietã, bell'idol mio" (Bellini); "M'ama, non m'ama" (Mascagni); "Notte" (Respighi); "A Vucchella" (Tosti); "O luna che fa lume" (Davico); pianist, Favaretto London 5394

The Artistry of Renata Tebaldi
"Addio del passato" (Verdi, *La Traviata*); "O patria mia" (Verdi, *Aïda*); "Willow Song", (Verdi, *Otello*); "Deh vieni, non tardar" (Mozart, *Le Nozze di Figaro*); "Mi chiamano Mimi," "Donde lieta usci" (Puccini, *La Bohème*) "Ebbene, ne andro lontano" (Catalani, *La Wally*); "L'altra notte" (Boito, *Mefistofele*); "La mamma morta" (Giordano, *Andrea Chenier*); conds. Basile, Rescigno, Sanzogno Everest Stereo 3438
Everest Mono 3205

Tebaldi in Stereo
"Per l'amor di Gesũ," "Grazie sorelle" (Refice, *Cecilia*); "Ne mai dunque avrõ la pace," (Catalani, *La Wally*); "Io son l'umile ancella," "Poveri fiori" (Cilea, *Adriana Lecouvreur*); "Porgi amor," "Dove sono" (Mozart, *Le Nozze di Figaro*); "Selva opaca" (Rossini, *Guillaume Tell*); "Flammen perdonami" (Mascagni, *Lodoletta*); cond. Erede London OS 25020

An Evening at the Chicago Lyric Opera
"La mamma morta" (Giordano, *Andrea Chenier*); "L'altra notte" (Bonito, *Mefistofele*); Letter Scene (Tchaikovsky, *Eugen Onegin*); "L'amo come il fulgor di creato" (with Simionato) (Ponchielli, *La Gioconda*); cond. Solti
London LL 1626

Operatic Arias
"Tu che le vanitã" (Verdi, *Don Carlos*); "Ecco l'orrido campo," "Morrò, ma prima in grazia" (Verdi, *Un Ballo in Maschera*); "Sempre all'alba" (Verdi, *Giovanni d'Arco*); "In questa reggia" (Puccini, *Turandot*); "Sogno di Doretta" (Puccini, *La Rondine*); "Suicidio" (Ponchielli, *La Gioconda*); "Voi lo sapete" (Mascagni, *Cavalleria Rusticana*); "Esser madre è un inferno" (Cilea, *L'Arlesiana*); cond. di Fabritiis London OS 25912

Tebaldi Festival
"Dich teure Halle," "Elisabeth's Prayer" (Wagner, *Tannhäuser*); "Elsa's Dream" (Wagner, *Lohengrin*); Liebestod (Wagner, *Tristan und Isolde*); Habañera, Card Scene (Bizet, *Carmen*); "Amour, viens aidez ma faiblesse," "Mon coeur s'ouvre a ta voix" (Saint-Saëns, *Samson et Dalila*); "Adieu, notre petite table," "Ne-c'est plus ma main" (Massenet, *Manon*); "Ritorna vincitor" (Verdi, *Aïda*); Musetta's Waltz (Puccini, *La Bohème*); "La regata veneziana" (Rossini); "Granada" (Lara, Poletto); "Estrellia" (Ponce); Catarí, Catarí" (Cardillo); "A vuchella" (Tosti); "Non ti scordar di me" (De Curtis); "If I Loved You" (Rodgers); conds. Guadagno, Bonynge 2-London OSA 1282

A Christmas Festival
"Adeste Fideles"; "Ave Maria (Bach, Gounod); Wiegenlied (Brahms); "What Child Is This?"; "O Holy Night" (Adam); "Tu scendi delle stelle"; "Silent Night"; "Panis Angelicus" (Franck); "O Divine Redeemer" (Gounod); "Mille cherubini in coro" (Schubert); "Ave Maria" (Schubert); cond. Guadagno London 0526241

Tebaldi in Concert
"Me voglio fa'na casa" (Donizetti); "La tua stella" (Mascagni); "Sogno" (Tosti); "L'invito" (Rossini); "L'assiuolo" (Zandonai); "Stornello" (Cimara); "Noi leggevamo insieme" (Ponchielli); "Serenata" (Mascagni); "Se tu m'ami" (Pergolesi); "M' ha preso alla sua ragna" (Paradisi); "O

cessate di pigarmi" (Scarlatti); "O del mio dolce ardor" (Gluck); "Il carretiere del Vomero" (Ricci); "La sposa del marinaro" (Marcadante); "Malinconia, ninfa gentile" (Bellini); "E L'uccelino" (Puccini); pianist, Bonynge London OS 26303

Great Love Duets (with Franco Corelli)

"Tu, tu amore, tu" (Puccini, *Manon Lescaut*); "L'abborita mia rivale" (Verdi, *Aïda*); "Dunque è vero (Cilea, *Adriana Lecouvreur*); "Deh non turbare (Ponchielli, *La Gioconda*); "No Smaragdi . . . Inghirlandata di violette" (Zandonai, *Francesca da Rimini*); cond. Guadagno London OS 26315

PIRATED RECITALS

Renata Tebaldi: Faust—Three Scenes; Verdi Requiem—Three Excerpts; Rossini—Stabat Mater—Inflammatus

Church Scene, Valentin's Death, Prison Scene (with Filippeschi, Savarese, Tajo, cond. Patane) (Gounod, *Faust*); "Ricordare," "Agnus Dei," "Libera Me" (Barbieri, cond. Toscanini) (Verdi, *Messa da Requiem*); "Inflammatus" (Rossini, *Stabat Mater*) Penzance Records #9

Tebaldi and Tucker—Great Scenes from La Forza del Destino, Simon Boccanegra, Andrea Chenier and Manon Lescaut

"Ah, per sempre, mia bell'anima" (Verdi, *La Forza del Destino);* Tu, tu amore, tu," Act Four from the beginning through "Sola, perduta, abbandonata" (Puccini, *Manon Lescaut*); Act One Duet (Verdi, *Simon Boccanegra*); "Ore soave," "La nostra morte" (Giordano, *Andrea Chenier*) ERR-104-1

ALBUMS CONTAINING EXCERPTS FROM COMPLETE RECORDINGS

The Best of Tebaldi

"Mi chiamano Mimi" (Puccini, *La Bohème*); "Vissi d'arte" (Puccini, *Tosca*); "Lassù nel Soledad" (Puccini, *La Fanciulla del West*); "Un bel dì" (Puccini, *Madama Butterfly*); "Signore ascolta," Death of Liù (Puccini, *Turandot*); La mamma morta (Giordano, *Andrea Chenier*); "Io son l'umile ancella," "Poveri fiori" (Cilea, *Adriana Lecouvreur*); "L'altra notte" (Boito, *Mefistofele*); conds. Serafin, Molinari-Pradelli, Capuana, Erede, Gavazzeni London OS 25729

Italian Opera Arias

"Signore ascolta," Death of Liù (Puccini, *Turandot*); "In quelle trine morbide" (Puccini, *Manon Lesçaut*); "Un bel di" (Puccini, *Madama Butterfly*); "Addio del passato" (Verdi, *La Traviata*); "Pace, pace mio Dio" (Verdi, *La Forza del Destino*); "L'altra notte" (Boito, *Mefistofele*); "La mamma morta" (Giordano, *Andrea Chenier*); conds. Erede, Molinari-Pradelli, Serafin, Gavazzeni London OS 25120

Famous Operatic Duets (with Mario Del Monaco)

"Pur ti riveggo," "La fatale pietra" (Verdi, *Aïda*); "Già nella notte densa," "Dio ti giocondi" (Verdi, *Otello*); "Tu, tu, amore tu" (Puccini, *Manon Lescaut*); conds. Erede, Molinari-Pradelli London 5175

Renata Tebaldi

Great Moments from Puccini Operas
"Senza mamma" *(Suor Angelica)*; "O Michele, Michele" *(Il Tabarro)*; "O mio babbino caro" *(Gianni Schicchi)*; "Un bel dì" *(Madama Butterfly)*; "Lassù nel Soledad" *(La Fanciulla del West)*; "Fa freddo . . . Entrate" *(La Bohème)*; conds. Gardelli, Serafin, Capuana London OS 25950

Renata Tebaldi's Greatest Hits
"Ritorna vincitor" (Verdi, *Aïda*); "Mi chiamano Mimi" (Puccini, *La Bohème*); "Vissi d'arte" (Puccini, *Tosca*); "Salce, salce . . . Ave Maria" (Verdi, *Otello*); "Io son l'umile ancella" (Cilea, *Andriana Lecouvreur*); "O mio babbino caro" (Puccini, *Gianni Schicchi*); "La mamma morta" (Giordano, *Andrea Chenier*); "Un bel dì" (Puccini, *Madama Butterfly*); "A Vucchella" (Tosti); "Non ti scordar di me" (De Curtis); conds. von Karajan, Serafin, Molinari-Pradelli, Capuana, Gavazzeni, Bonynge London OS 26348

Tebaldi in Duets
"Lontano, lontano" (with Del Monaco) (Boito, *Mefistofele*); "Sono andate, fingeva di morire" (with Bergonzi) (Puccini, *La Bohème*); "Viene la sera" (with Bergonzi) (Puccini, *Madama Butterfly*); "Tu sei la corona" (with Del Monaco) (Cilea, *Adriana Lecouvreur*); "Hai ragione, è un tormento" (with Del Monaco) (Puccini, *Il Tabarro*); "O dolci mani" (with Del Monaco) (Puccini, *Tosca*); conds. Serafin, Capuana, Gardelli, Molinari-Pradelli London OS 25951

Verdi Arias
"Tacea la notte . . . Di tale amor," "D'amor sull'ali rosee . . . Misere . . . Tu vedrai che amore in terra" *(Trovatore)*; "Me pellegrina ed orfana," "Son giunta! Grazie, o Dio . . . Madre pietosa Vergine" *(La Forza del Destino)*; "Salce, salce . . . Ave Maria" *(Otello)*; conds. Erde, Molinari-Pradelli London OS 25082